Leisure Arts 17

Working with Pastel

Christopher Stones

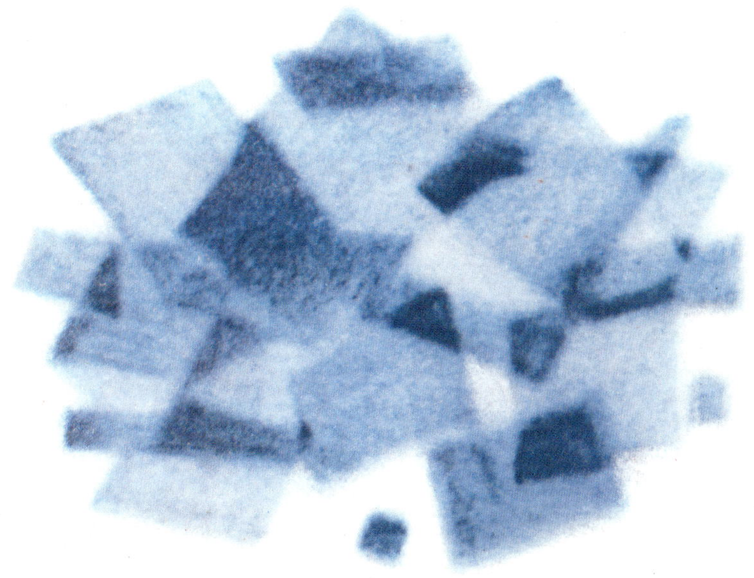

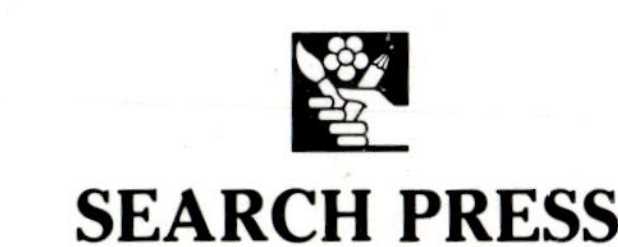

SEARCH PRESS

Wellwood North Farm Road Tunbridge Wells

The pastel medium

Pastel is a medium comparatively little known by the public but it certainly is not new. The majority of cave paintings are composed of compressed powder pigment, either calcinated or occurring naturally, and so pastel may well be considered the oldest painting medium. It is closely related to conté, which has been used by painters for centuries.

Pastel came into prominence in its present form in the seventeenth and eighteenth centuries, when its ability to produce incisive clarity as well as infinite sensitivity was exploited to the full. In eighteenth-century France pastel was considered as important as oil, and in the hands of the court painter, Maurice Quentin de la Tour, it reached its peak of popularity. La Tour claimed that whatever anyone could paint in any other medium he could do better in pastel. The use of pastel declined in the nineteenth century, being mostly used by painters as a delicate tint added to fine pencil or conté drawing, and it was usually applied with a sharpened pulp stub. This is the origin of the term pastel shades. The Impressionists made liberal use of pastel as a means of capturing a fleeting moment on paper. With deft light strokes pastel is ideal for the quick impression, but few painters thought of pastel as more than a lightning sketch medium for collecting notes or roughing in a trial composition.

This legacy of the Victorian and Impressionist painters lingers. Until recently the only use of pastel was by the amateur, and then only in the sketch tradition rather than as a full medium. But in the last ten years there has been a renaissance. Now at last the realisation has come that pastel, used as a full painting medium can have equal aggressive power as oil or acrylic, and as much subtlety and sensitivity as watercolour. The preconceived ideas of what a pastel painting should look like are gradually being broken down, and many progressive and experimental painters are taking it seriously and discovering its possibilities.

Throughout this book, I refer to *paint* and *painting* with pastel, for it is about pastel as a painting medium. Pastel drawing is outside the scope of this book. Think of pastel as dry paint – and you will begin to discover – and enjoy – the seemingly endless possibilities of this exciting medium.

Permanence

Artists' soft pastel is a very fine chalk ground with pigment and bound lightly into sticks with gum tragacanth. The general impression is that pastel, being just a powder, must be a fugitive, highly vulnerable medium with little permanence. It is true that until it is framed under glass a pastel painting is liable to smudging and paint loss but, once protected, it has proved itself more durable than other media; for pastel, being an inert opaque powder set on the surface of paper, will remain the same for hundreds of years without cracking, browning or foxing from damp or impurities, so long as it is protected from dust and grime.

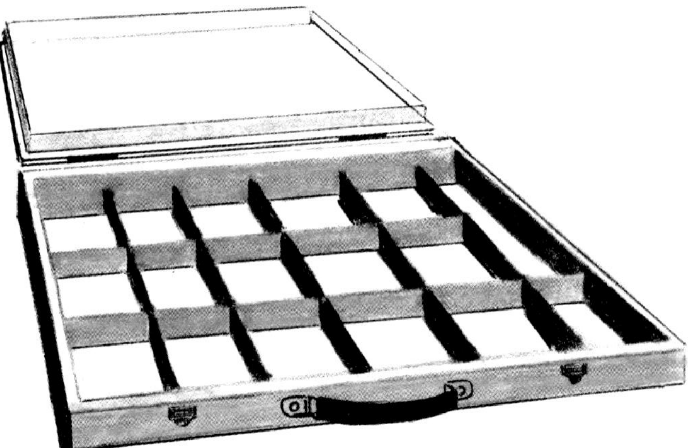

Fixatives

Fixatives are used to bind a pastel painting onto its supporting surface but experience shows that they ultimately impair permanence. When fixed, some pigments lighten and others darken; some become warmer and others colder in hue, and this can upset the interaction between colours. Fixatives do to some extent impair the surface glow or bloom of a pastel painting, making it flatter. However, there are times during the course of painting when it is useful to set part of the underpainting and apply unfixed strokes on top. This is described further on page 14. There are however various methods of using fixatives which can prove less drastic in certain cases, and these are discussed on page 30. Charcoal, being so much lighter in weight and easily blown or knocked off, *does* need to be fixed, especially if used as a drawing aid before applying pastel, for it can taint the lighter colours applied over it.

In the mid-eighteenth century several painters experimented with fixatives. Their fixed paintings have survived reasonably well but the unfixed ones remain as if they were painted yesterday.

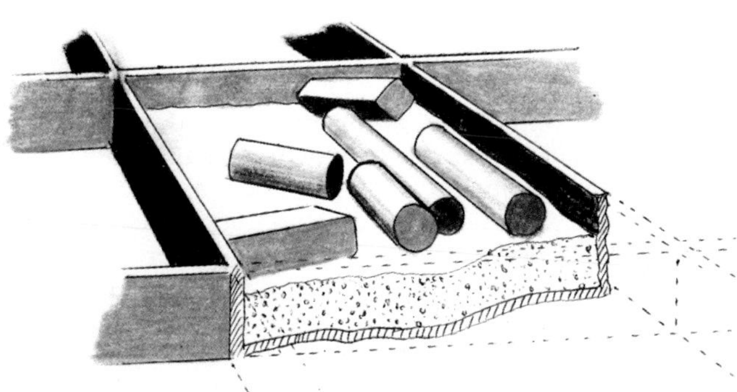

Choice of materials

If you have not used pastels before and are trying to buy some do take care to ask for Artists' Soft Pastels. Numerous products on the market are described as pastels, but they are not of the soft powdery variety. Many are bound with wax or oil, and while they are a respectable medium in their own right they fall outside the scope of this book. The individual makes of soft pastels do vary enormously in the quantity of binder used to keep them in stick form, the softest being so lightly bound that they break into powder when unwrapped or when they are knocked. The most heavily bound are usually of students' quality and can be so hard that I have torn the paper with them.

Pastel is basically a very fine cosmetic chalk mixed with pigment, and so it follows that the palest colours will feel the softest, having a large quantity of chalk, while the darkest colours are mostly pigment and can feel rather gritty, depending on the pigment used, so there is some variation in a single brand range. The choice of the medium – soft or very soft – is essentially a personal one, and depends on the paper used and the type of work you are doing. There is no point in trying to press very hard to make a clear staccato shape if you have a very soft pastel – it will just disintegrate! I use all consistencies of pastel and add to my range some small conté sticks which are square in section. I also occasionally use pastel pencils.

When you start to use pastel it is worth experimenting on sugar paper or any cheap rough support to see the kind of marks you can make: the light granular stroke with the side of the pastel; the varied pressure of stroke; rubbing an area in completely and putting a light granular and unrubbed stroke of contrasting tone over it; seeing how misty an image you can get one moment, and how clear and sharp at another. On the next pages I show four of the most widely used types of paper that pastellists choose.

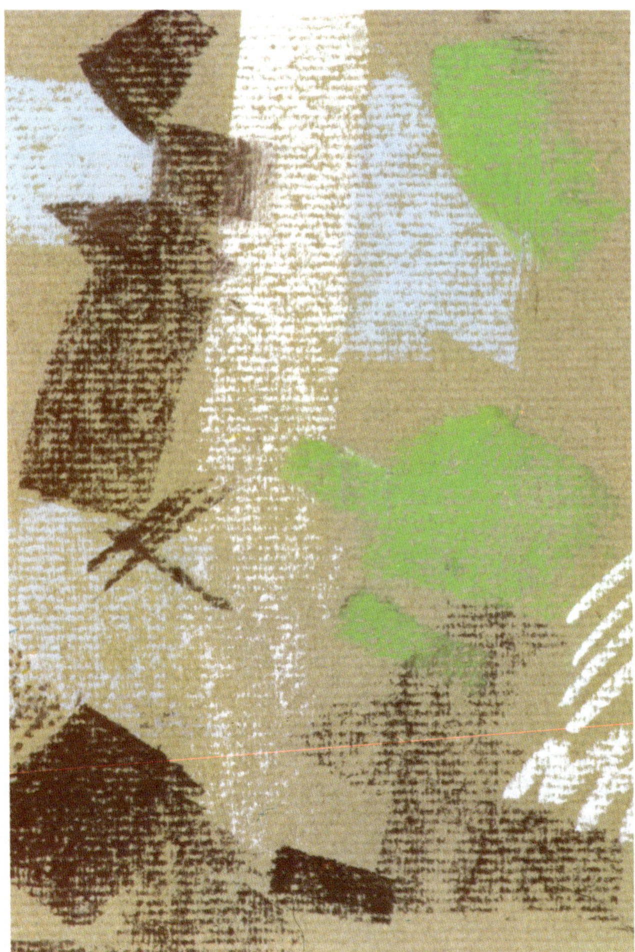

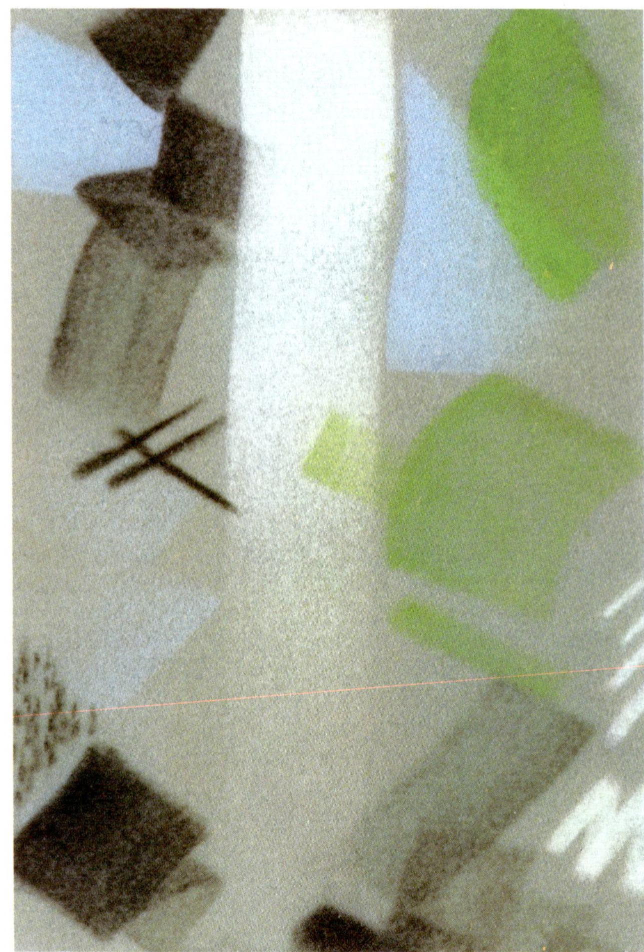

Ingres (Fabriano) paper

This is one of the most widely used papers for the traditional approach to pastel. Normally the picture is built up with light pressure strokes, allowing the grain of the paper to show through. Great care is taken to choose an appropriate colour of paper for the subject. For best results very little overlaying and intermixing of colours is done and hardly any touching in with the finger. Because you cannot blend colours together so readily you need many more different tones of each colour in your box. (See page 7.)

Velour paper

This has a furry surface, and is widely used in Europe. When painted, it gives a sensuous soft image, but is not capable of providing great clarity. It is better not to mix colours on it, so you need a large number of pastels, but as they wear down so slowly on this paper they last much longer. Velour paper is made in a range of colours, and is usually allowed to show through in places in the finished painting. (See page 10.)

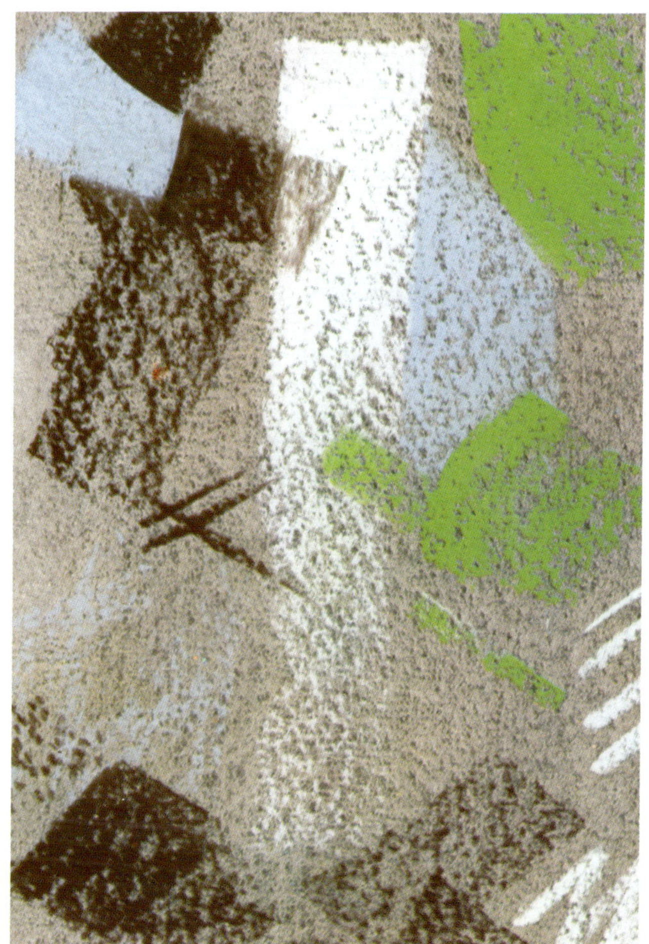

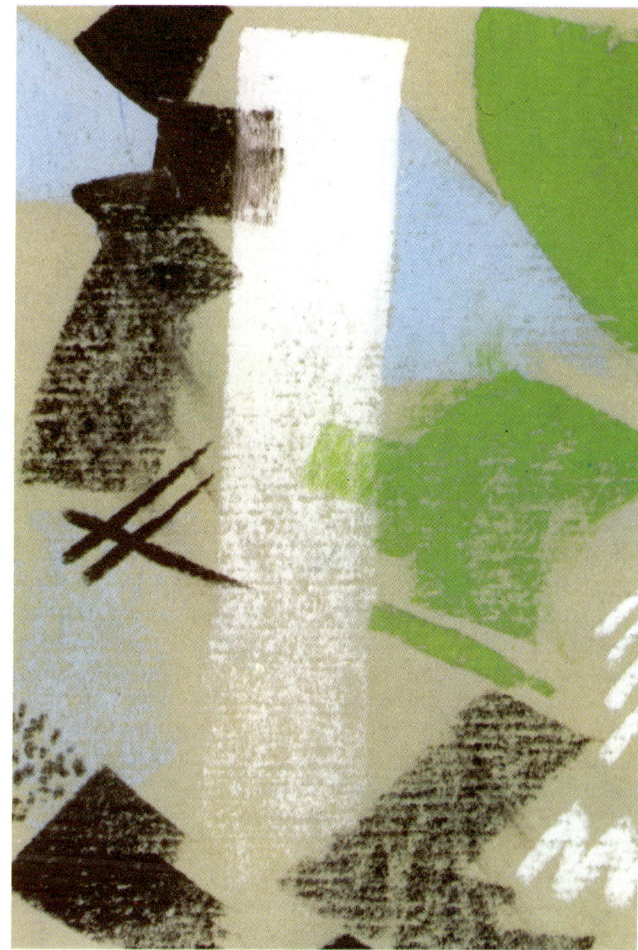

Watercolour paper

Watercolour paper is normally primed with an acrylic wash, which both tints it to the desired colour and toughens the surface. This surface is Bockingford NOT. The primed colour shows through the light strokes of pastel as in the first example, and again there is no finger work in the traditional approach to pastel. It is excellent for impression or sketch approach to painting with pastels. The rougher the paper the more difficult it is to fill the surface with pastel to achieve a fully worked block of colour. (See page 18.)

Sand-grain paper

This is my own personal preference. The quality I like best – glass paper – is normally used by woodworkers for finishing and smoothing wood surfaces. The 'tooth' holds each mark I make ideally, and allows perfect clarity of image as well as the subtlety of edge available to the oil painter; and because colours can be blended on the paper all the soft gradations of a watercolour wash are possible. You need a smaller range of colours, but you use them up faster. Mind your fingers! (See page 14.)

Organisation and care of materials

Until recently there has been no satisfactory working box for pastels on the market. Unless people have made their own they have managed with the display boxes which each manufacturer supplies with sets of pastels. Sticks of pastels are sold in tones graded from dark to light with names that are often unique to each manufacturer apart from the obvious cobalts, cadmiums and ochres, which are common to all, although the system of tones may vary. I find it impossible to work with pastels arrayed like a row of soldiers, each with its allotted niche to which it has to be returned after use. A pastel paintbox needs general compartments for yellows, reds, greys, blues and greens with subdivisions into two or three compartments for light, medium and dark (*see diagram on page 2*). I strip all paper coverings off the pastels before they go into my box, keeping a note of the make, name and number on a colour chart for re-ordering. Each compartment has a thin mattress of plastic foam (removable for cleaning) at the base, and a thicker piece of foam rubber covers the entire box, so that with the lid down the pastels are effectively sandwiched between foam and cannot jump about, sullying each other or being damaged.

The advantage of removing the wrapping paper is that you cannot work according to recipes. There are then no names or numbers on the pastels and you have to judge for yourself the relative warm and cool or light and dark of the colours, which is what the painting is all about. If you are uncertain about using a colour, try out the stick of pastel on a piece of scrap paper of the same colour, before finally committing yourself.

My box also contains a small compartment for a few pastel pencils, and a place for poster-mounting putty or material for sticking up posters and notices where one cannot drive in a pin. Apart from its original use it is ideal for the pastellist. If you keep a piece of this putty in your hands and knead it as you work it will keep your hands clean (and so your face and clothes too!). It stops you passing colour from a stick of pastel that you have just used to the next, and this keeps them clean longer. It also replaces the oils in your hands and nails which, by constant contact with such a powdery substance, can sometimes dry out and crack. You can also use it for lifting out an area of your picture which needs to be repainted, having first flicked out a thick application of pastel with an oil painting hog brush.

Your paper should be pinned, clipped or taped to a drawing board so that it lies flat. If it is not ready-mounted on stiff card or is fairly thin, you will need several sheets beneath it to cushion any imperfections that may come through from the board. For working out-of-doors a light but firm easel is advisable as, when working on your knee, it is difficult to prevent your sleeve getting in the paint. If you do not want to sit on a stool you may still need one on which to rest the pastel box at a reachable height from a standing position.

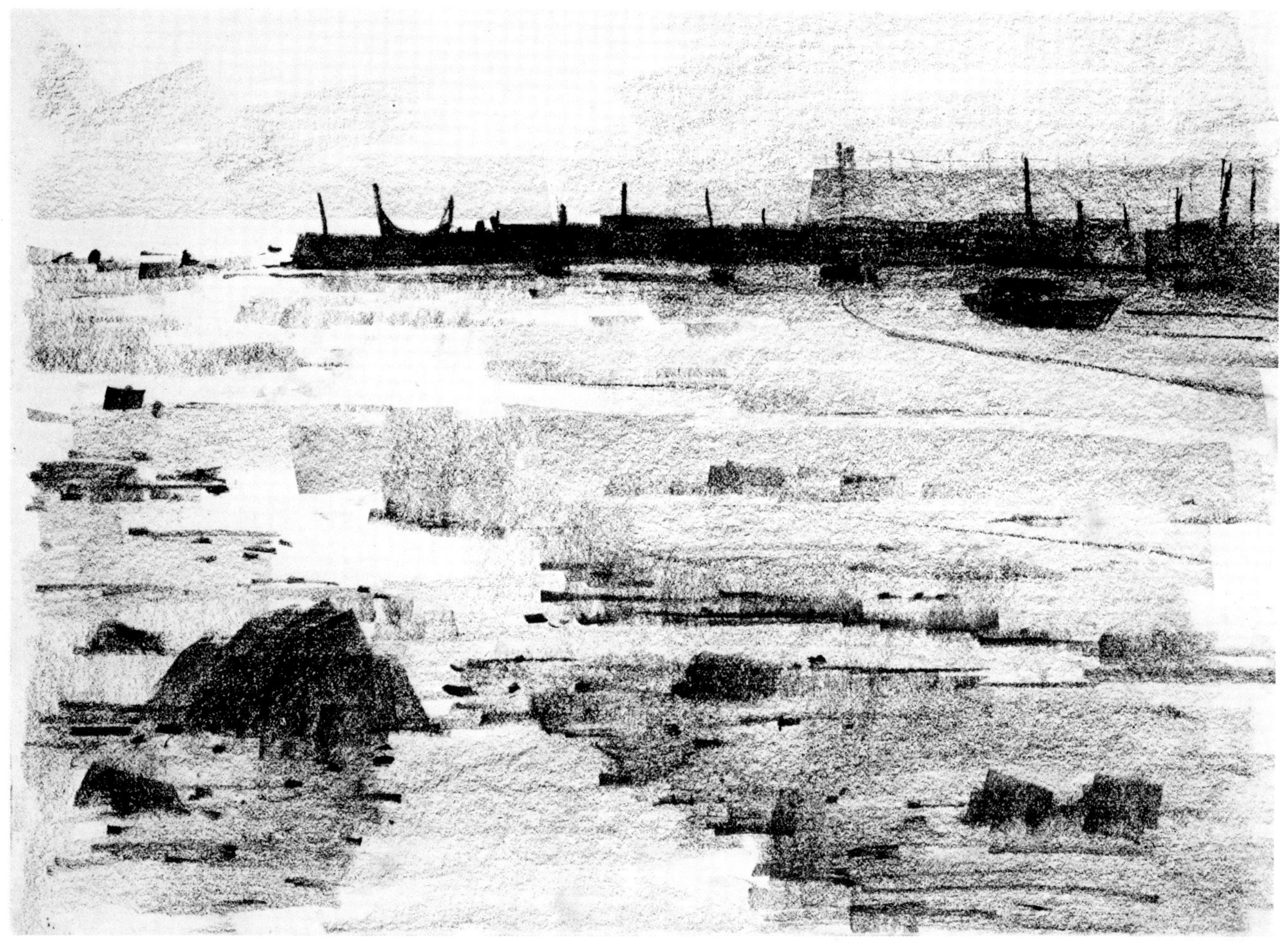

Seashore: demonstration

Jersey, Channel Islands

Painted on Ingres (Fabriano) paper

I like to make a tonal study before starting the actual painting because I can determine the composition, the relative intensity of lights and darks, and make any alterations to my first ideas at this stage. Here I have blocked it in in conté on white cartridge paper, but any scrap of paper will do – even the back of an envelope. I was interested in the wet sand at low tide, and wanted to draw the eye to the staccato form of the breakwater and the water running out towards it.

Stage 1 (page 8)

I lay in the principal darks and lights on a sandy coloured paper with very light pressure strokes, using the side of the pastels. In this traditional approach I choose a coloured paper that will be of advantage when

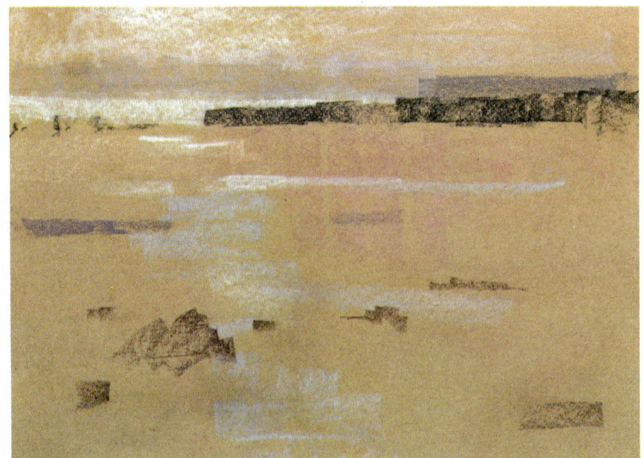
Stage 1

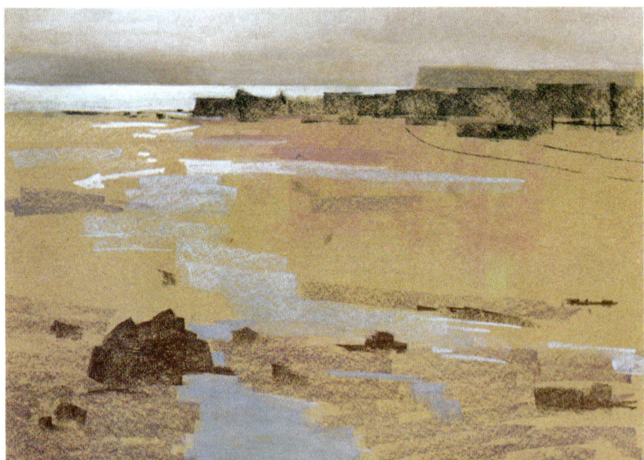
Stage 2

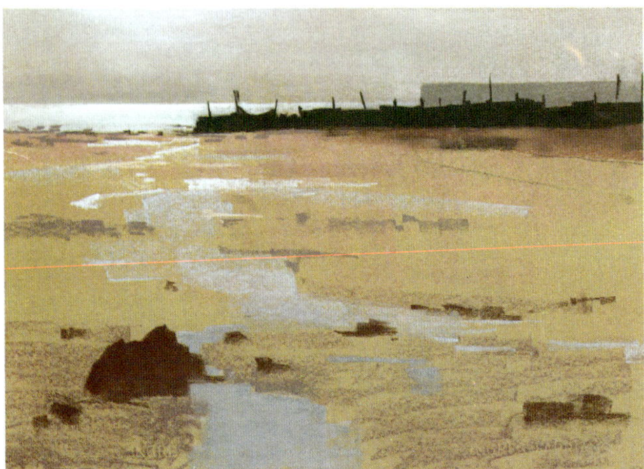
Stage 3

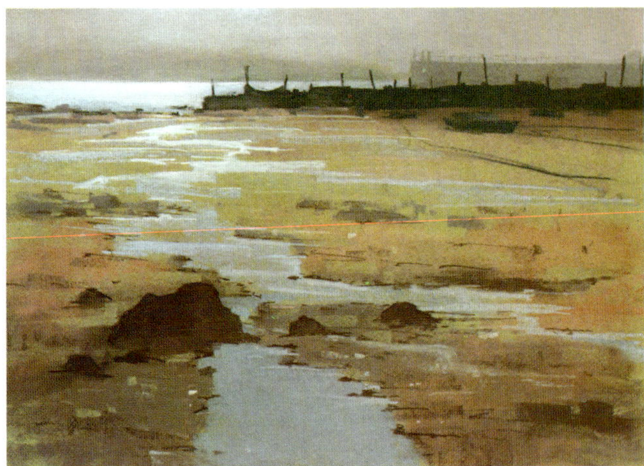
Stage 4 – the finished painting

partially left showing in the final painting. I enjoy the freedom of just blocking in the shapes with no preliminary line work, but you might be happier starting with some light drawing before applying pastel.

Stages 2–3

Generally this is a consolidation of the previous stage, but I feel the need to eliminate the sandy colour of the paper from the sea and sky. I lay thick strokes of pastel in this area and rub it in, carefully emphasising the horizontal of light water. A warm dark is used to modify the general tone of the foreground.

Paying but little attention to the foreground at this stage, I concentrate my efforts on the exact formation of the breakwater and the water's edge, and in laying in the colours of the distant sand.

Stage 4 – the finished painting

Apart from adding small details of boats and the distant jetty, in this final stage I describe the wet sand and the

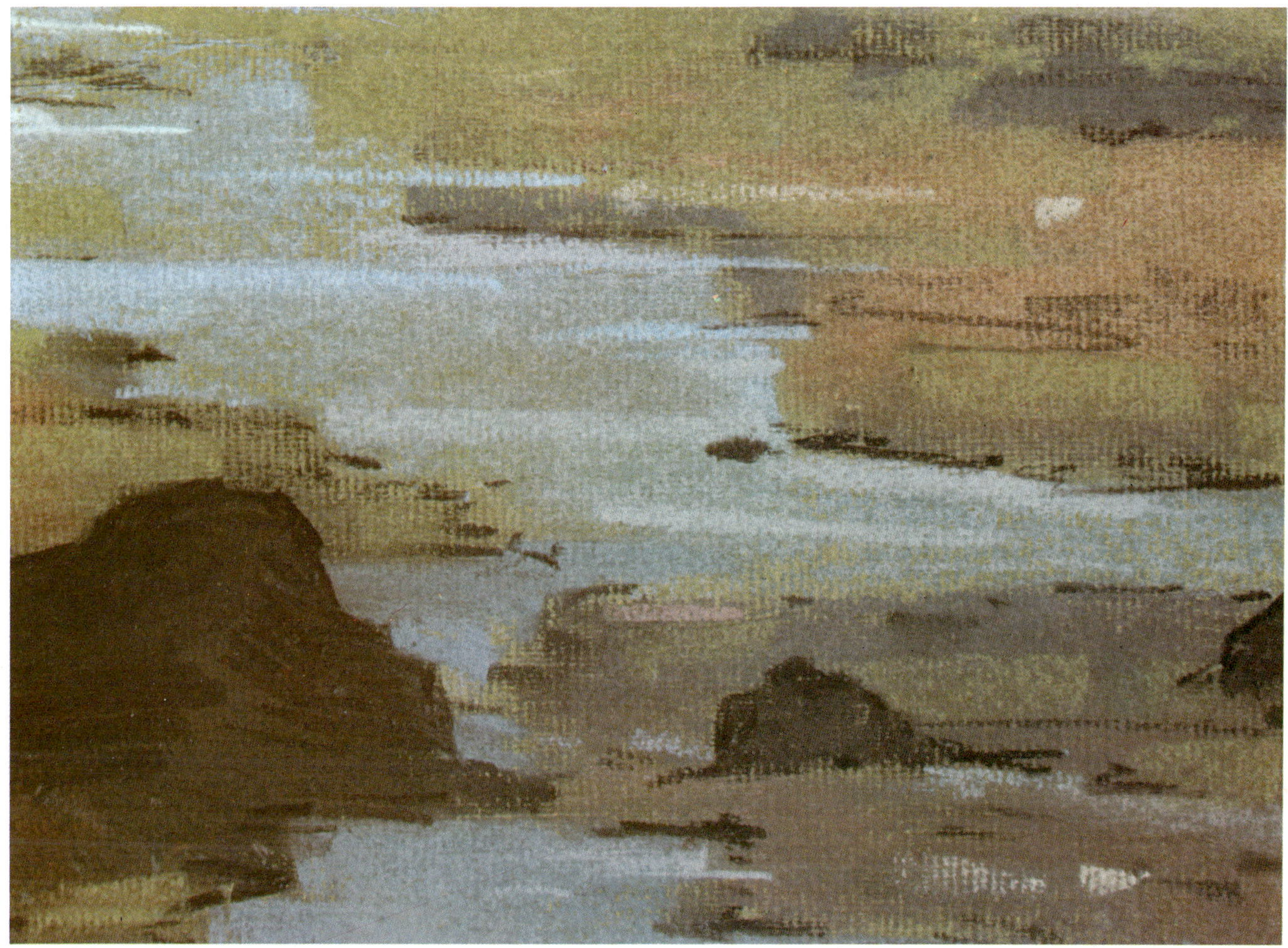

Detail (actual size)

rivulets of water running back to the sea. I make sure that no light/dark contrast vies with that of the sea and breakwater, and that I do not overwork the immediate foreground, which could make it look laboured and attract too much attention.

Seashore detail (*shown above – actual size*)

This 'detail' shows the strokes and the mark making in the picture. Many pastellists like to let the grain of the paper show through the painting, but I like the variety of texture that is made by the interaction of the smooth and granular areas. In the foreground I felt the need to work a full layer of colour into the paper with my fingers before overlaying the lighter and darker surface detail, which went in with no further rubbing or finger-work. The resulting surface is an interplay of sharp and soft edges. Most fine detail is inserted with small fragments of pastel, but I do occasionally use some bistre coloured conté for dark accents and edges.

Flowers: demonstration

Painted on flock/velour paper

This is an interesting paper on which to work, which is used a great deal in Europe. It produces a sensuously soft image, and gives best results with the softest brands of pastel. Its advantages lie in the fact that it uses up the pastel very economically, and it encourages a very deft approach to painting, although it is difficult to erase mistakes. It is useful to have a good range of colours and tones because there is a limit to mixing on it.

Do not mix with your fingers on this paper, but work one colour in and put a firm stroke of another colour on top. Rubbing with the fingers does not help the colours to blend further. There is a pleasing subtlety and sensitivity in almost any work done on this paper, although it is less suitable for subjects where a very sharply defined image is intended.

When using flock paper, try not to fill the surface of the paper too soon. If you do so, it quickly becomes clogged, and you may have to brush some out with a dry, clean oil painting brush. It is better if you build up gradually to the required density of pastel layer as you become more decided about the exact forms that you want.

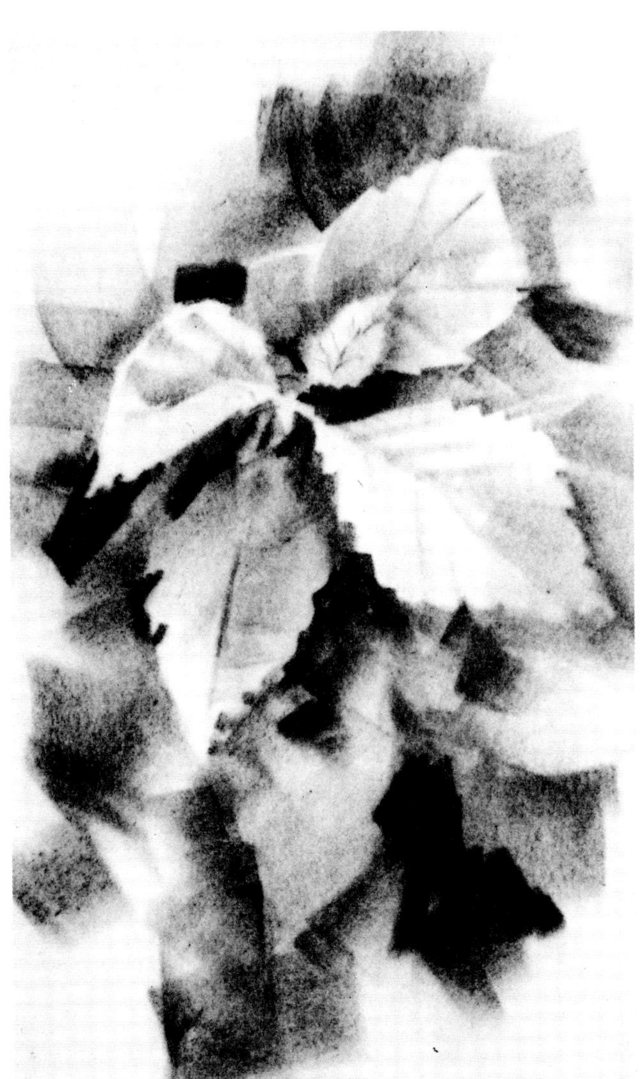

Leaves – a tonal study on velour/flock paper.

Stage 1 (page 12)

Having done a tone study to decide on the composition I wanted my first stage to establish the basic positions of the flowerheads, ignoring the actual spiky character of each head but trying to determine the different directions they were facing, and to make sure that there was enough variety of size and colour variation. The flowers were growing naturally, and I wanted to catch the informality of the shapes that they made by using some that were turning away from me and suggesting some distant blooms.

Stage 2

Next, using the flat edge of the pastel sticks, I lightly block in the darks in the background in order to describe the contours of the light flowers. I use light strokes so as not to overload the paper with colour and to allow me to add more colours later. I use deep green in the lower part of the picture and a blue-grey higher up. This begins to suggest distance and volume.

Stage 3

I continue to sharpen the image by filling in the background more solidly with the beginning of leaf shapes. Light areas on the selected flowerheads is stressed and the other flowers darkened. I develop the modelling more clearly, particularly in the centre of interest.

Detail (actual size)

Only now do I really clarify the image fully in the centre-right portion of the picture. Most of the work of forming detail is done with the ends of the pastel sticks. The paper will not accept any very great detail of modelling.

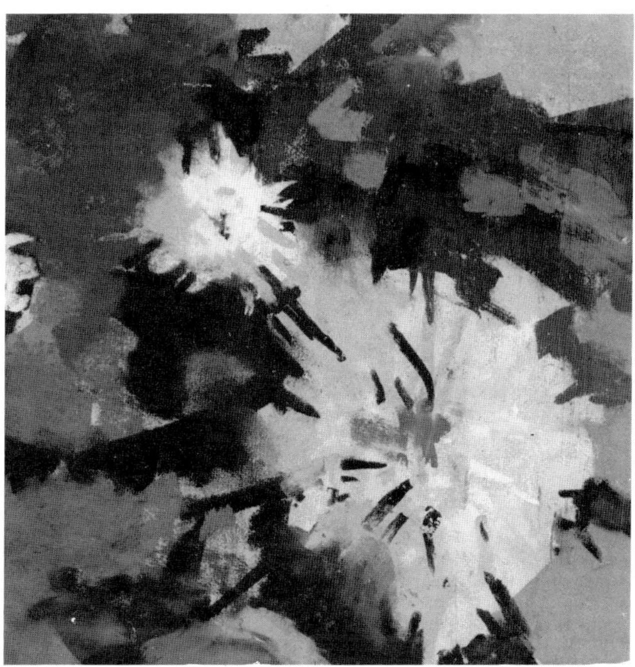

Flower heads and foliage. *Another study, reproduced here in monochrome but printed in colour on the front cover of this book.*

Stage 4 – the finished painting

I check the relative importance of individual flowers so that the less important blooms do not vie for attention. I then decide on just how much modelling I want in the foliage in the foreground and accent it accordingly.

Stage 1

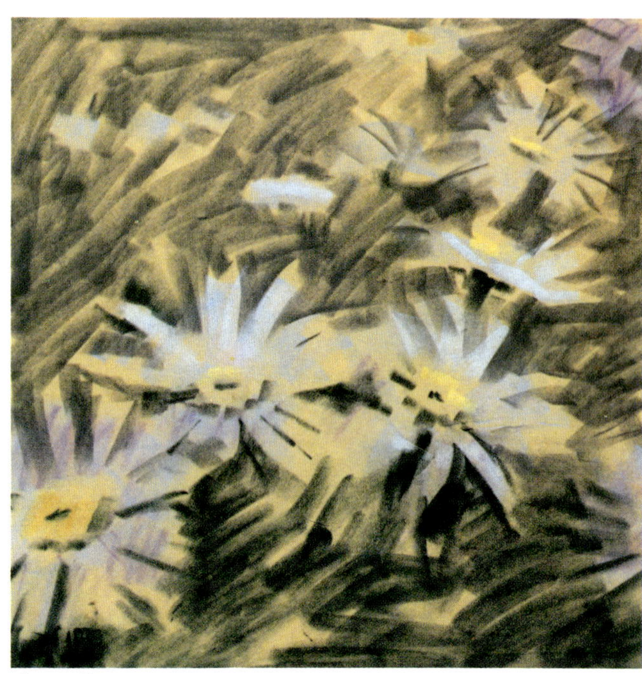

Stage 2

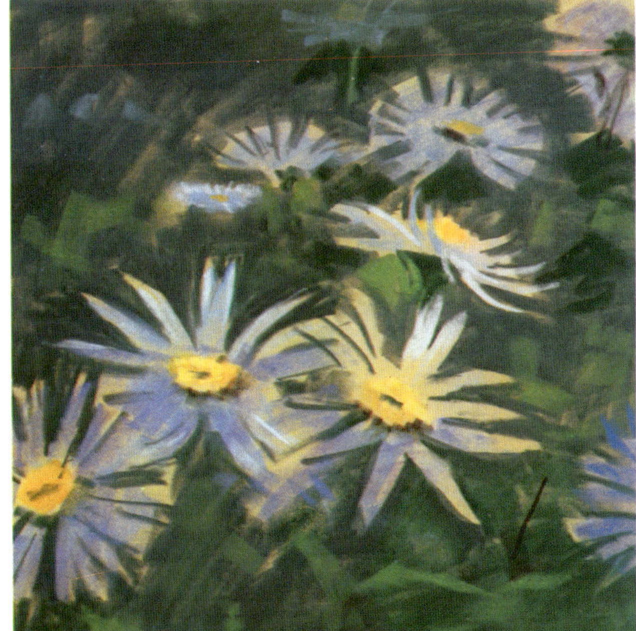

Stage 3

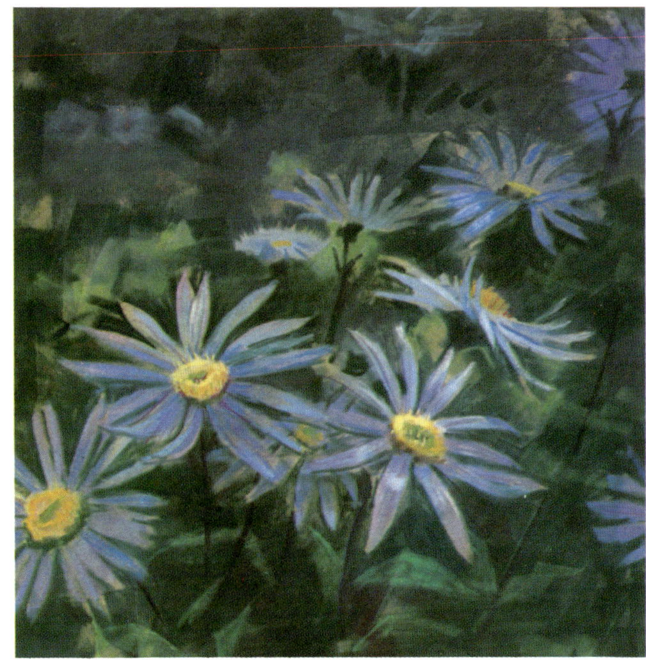

Stage 4 – the finished painting

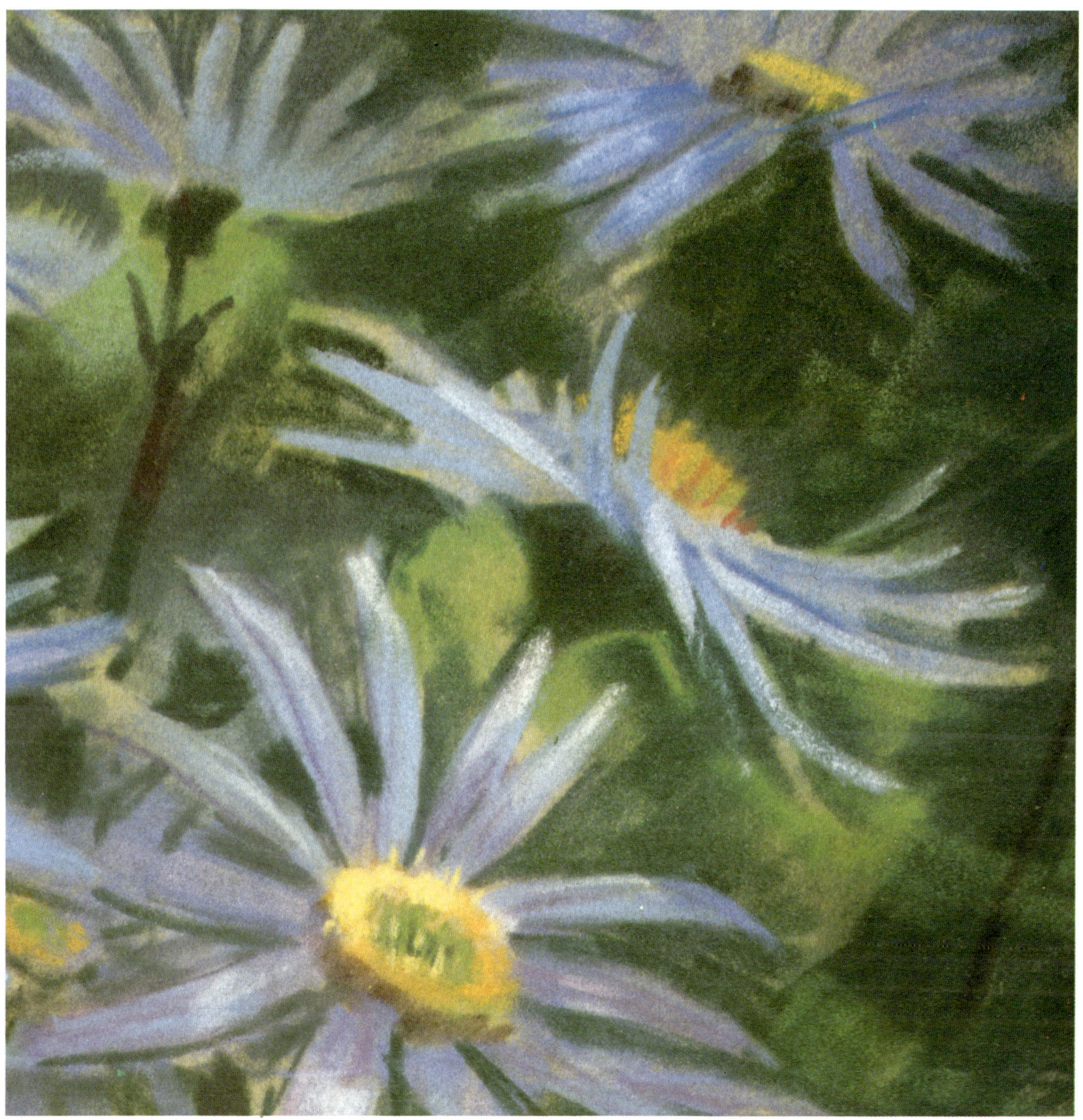

Detail (actual size)

'Storm clouds': a detail from the painting is reproduced on the back cover.

Using sand-grained paper

If you build up a pastel painting, filling the surface of the paper fully, as Pastellists did in the seventeenth and eighteenth centuries, you need a paper which does not easily become clogged up, one that allows the full range of sharpness and softness to be shown, and one on which you can build up a range of textures that will help to describe form. The old hand-made papers had an open pore structure that could hold the pigment, and were more able to accept the full load of colour applied to it than can our modern machine-made pastel papers. A modern alternative is very fine woodworking sandpaper, which holds the pastel admirably. I have also tried the waterproof 'wet and dry' abrasive papers, but these do not hold the pastel as well and tend to shed the colour. I find that 00 grade sandpaper or glasspaper is ideal for my purpose. I use commercially made sandpaper, but you can make your own with granite dust or fine sand applied to a gummed board.

As you might imagine a sand-grained support does use up your pastels very fast, but I find that the quality of image that can be made is such an improvement on the traditional papers that it is well worth using.

I cannot over-emphasise that if you are mean with your colour sticks and try to rub insufficient pastel into the paper, you will only wear out the skin on your fingers and soon pay for your miserliness – in blood! If you ensure that you have enough pastel on the surface before smoothing it in with your fingers the mix will survive intact.

With sand-grained paper you can achieve a perfectly smooth, clean area of colour yet make it sharply defined against an adjacent colour, even if it is one you have blended from three or four different pastel sticks. You can build up colours that no manufacturer has yet made and if you blend further all the colours together fully with your fingers it is impossible to make the result look muddy – it simply becomes a different colour.

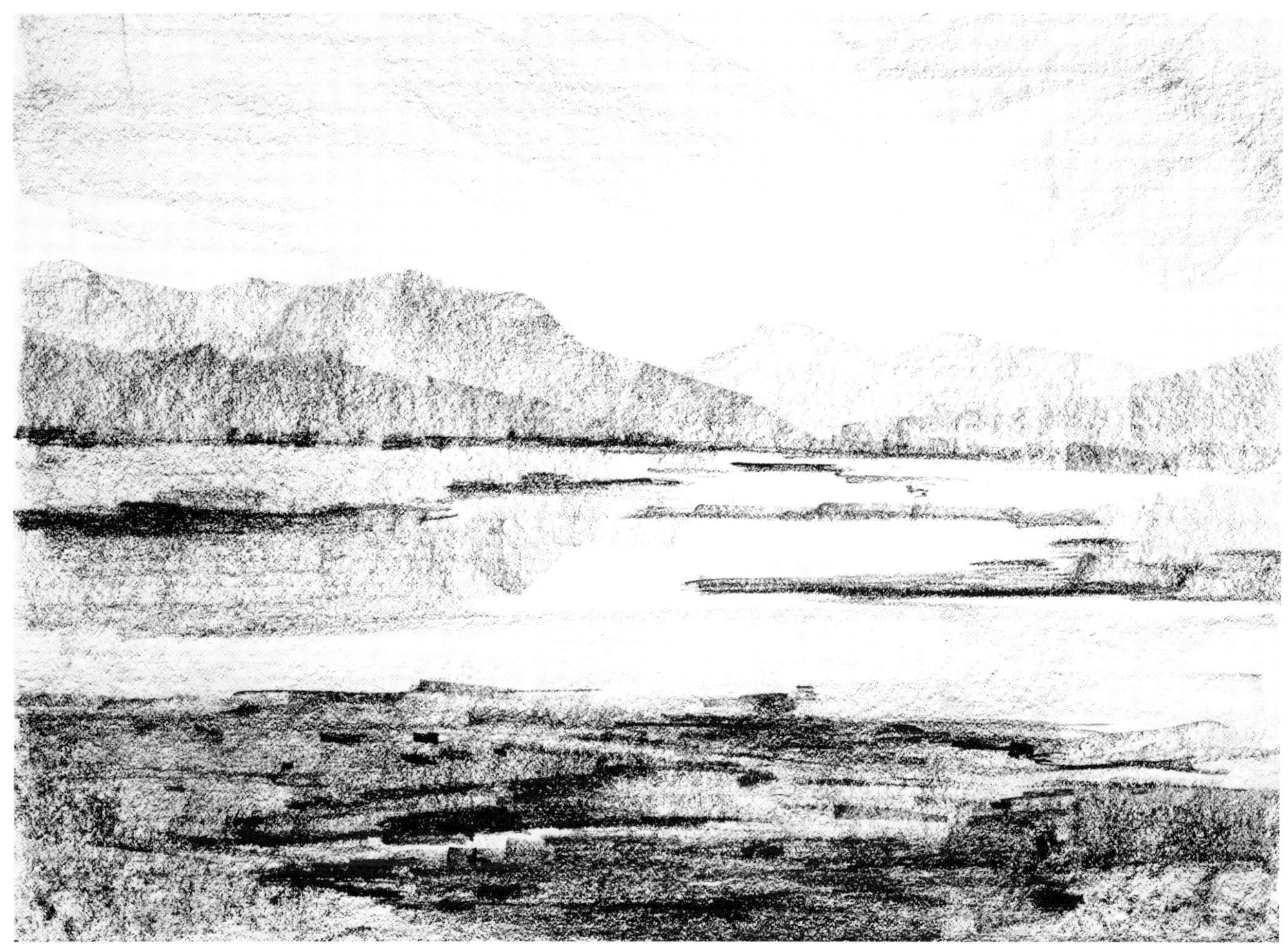

Porthmadog Estuary: demonstration

Demonstration on sandpaper

Once on my way to North Wales I was struck in the late afternoon by a wonderful vista of the mountains of Snowdonia with the still water of the estuary and the wet mud in the foreground. The sky was very simple with a glow of light low above the horizon. With the broken forms and texture there was in the area of mud in the foreground, it struck me that it was an exciting potential conflict of interest between the mud and the distance, which could be resolved in pictorial form.

Stage 1 (page 16)

I start by deciding on the relative distribution of sky to land in my tonal study and begin the painting by placing this in light strokes on the sandpaper, but at this stage nowhere filling the grain of the paper.

Stage 1

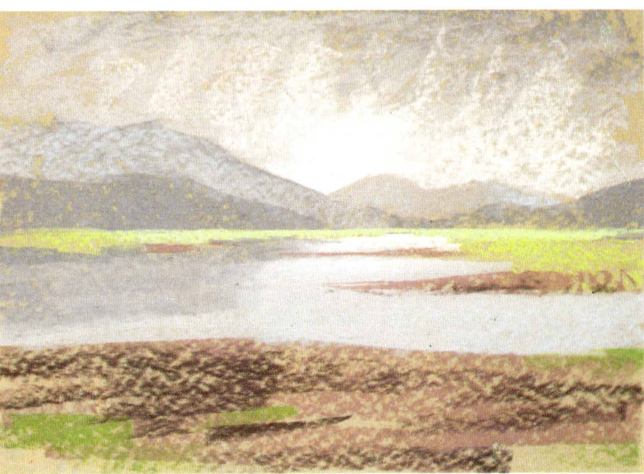
Stage 2

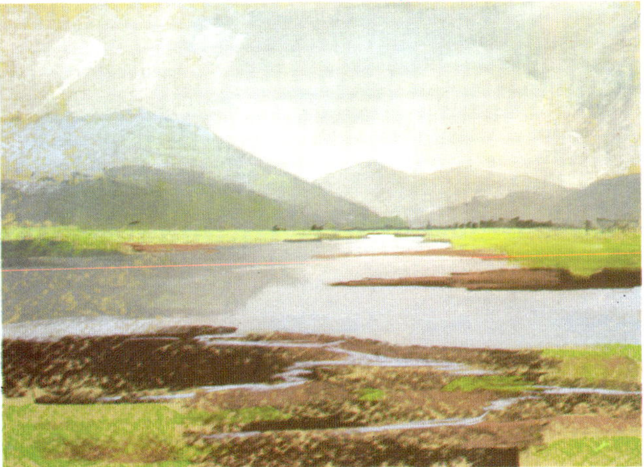
Stage 3

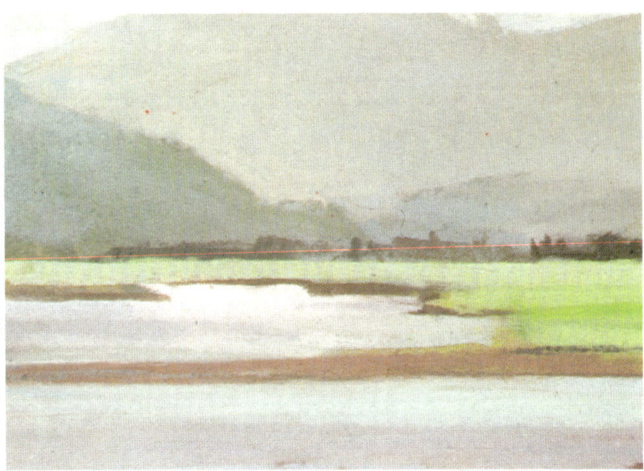
Detail (actual size)

Stage 2

Gradually I complete the lay-in in light strokes. Once the main areas are blocked in I fill the water and parts of the distance in with further strokes, smoothing the colours with my finger tips into flat areas. Do not try to rub in too soon when there is insufficient pastel on the surface, otherwise you will wear the skin off the end of your fingers. Always ensure that there is enough pastel filling the grain of the paper.

Stage 3

I decide to complete the upper central area of the painting in order to judge how much emphasis to give the foreground mud without it dominating the painting. Normally I would not allow myself to complete one area of a painting before the rest was in step, but it is useful to do so when there is a possible conflict between two or more areas of the composition.

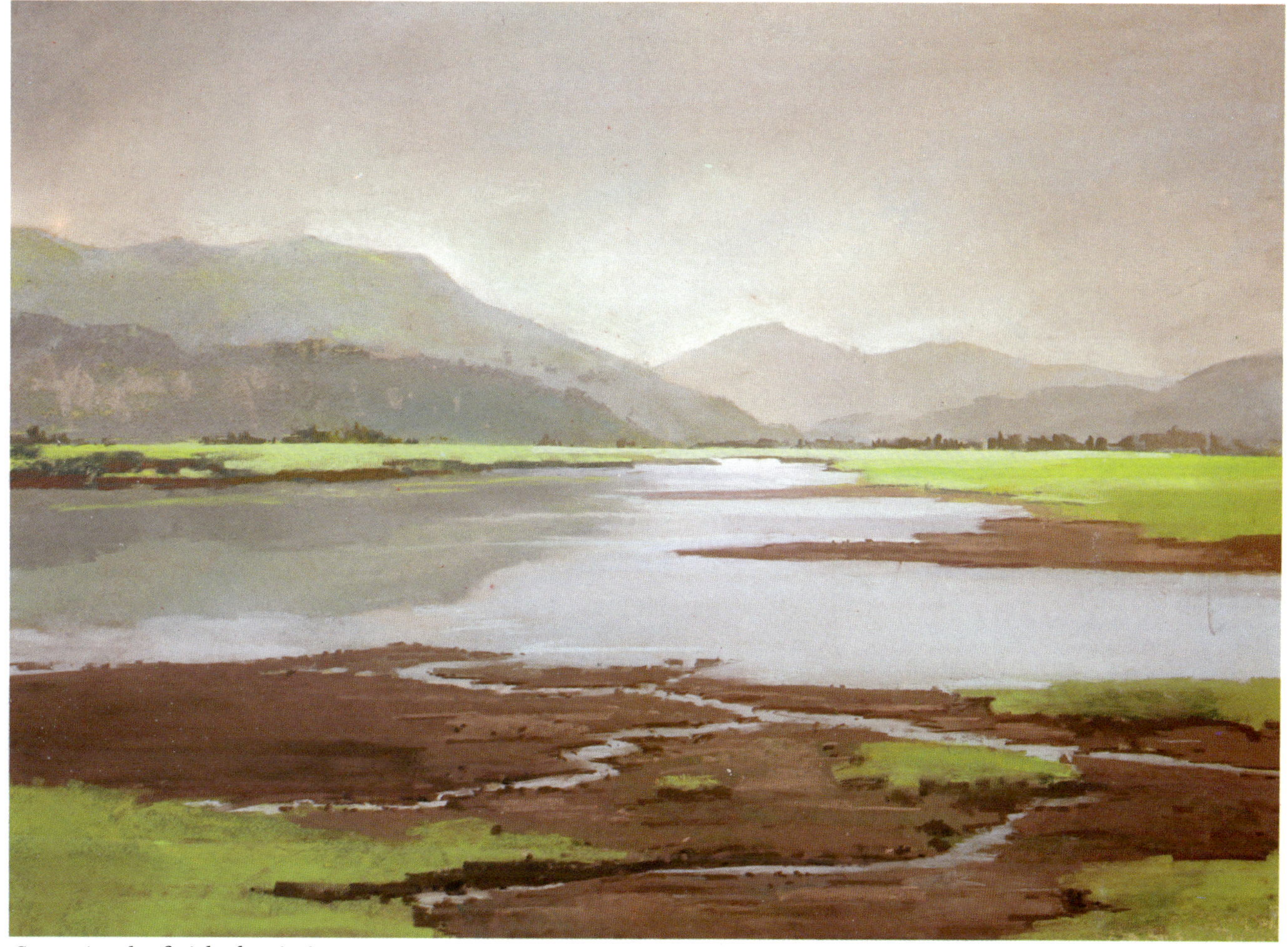

Stage 4 – the finished painting

Stage 4 – the finished painting

Having done this I can work outwards and downwards, bringing the picture to completion as shown in the illustration of the finishing painting.

Detail (actual size)

In this close-up of the centre-right portion of the painting you can see how fully loaded the paper is, and also that I like to cover all the paper. This means that I employ the full impact of one colour against another, with the possibility of varying the sharpness of edge between colours. The colours I end up with are often a mixture of several individual pastel sticks, each stroked on in turn and worked in together with my fingers.

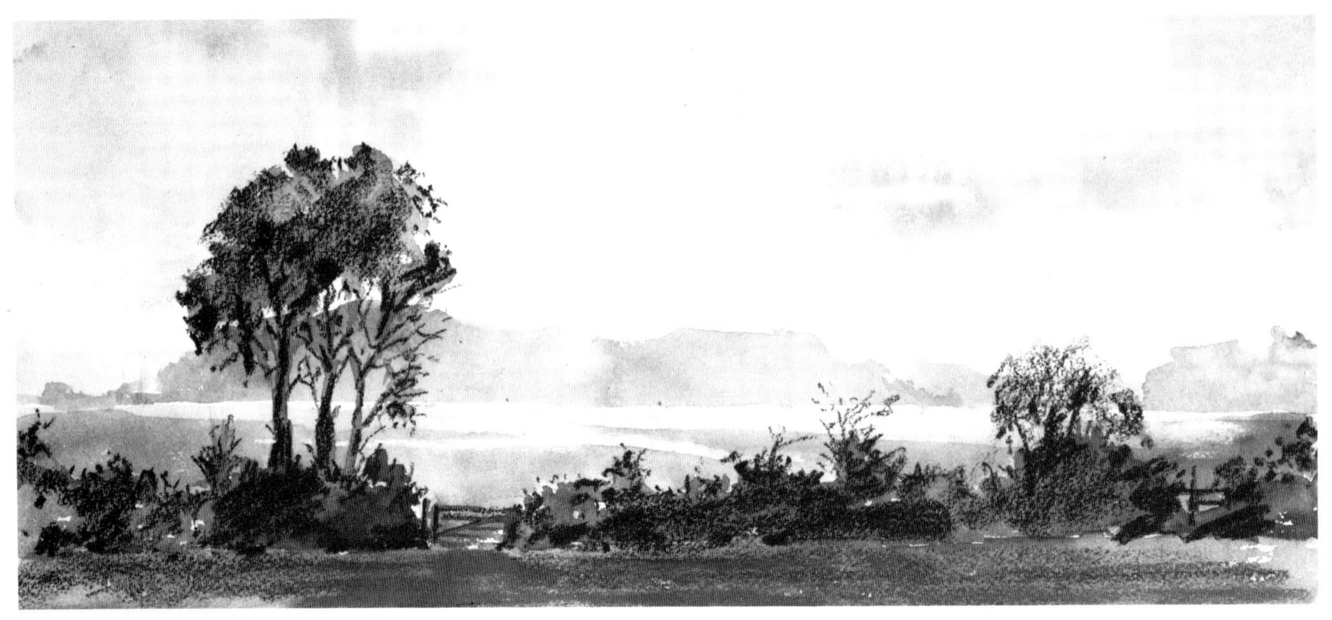

Pastel with other media

There is some controversy among practising artists as to whether it is legitimate to use other media, such as gouache or watercolour, as an underpainting for a pastel. The purists believe that pastel should never be used except on its own, and that any other material – especially a wet medium – applied with it, is reprehensible. Others consider that it does not really matter how you achieve a result, so long as it 'works'. There is almost every degree of opinion between these two, but personally I have rarely felt the need to mix media because I have found using pastel alone, with the occasional addition of conté, sufficient to create any image that I have asked of it.

Many painters use a watercolour paper, which they prime with acrylic paint to the required colour. This toughens the surface which might otherwise begin to disintegrate when pastel is worked into it. Usually parts of this primer are allowed to show through in the finished painting. Others take this priming a stage further, by colouring different areas (for instance sky and ground in a landscape) so that both show through. If you extend this preliminary technique still further and make a block layout of your composition you can well use watercolour or water-based inks as an underpainting rather than acrylic as a primer. The more elaborate the underpainting is, the less the paper needs to be toughened because the overlay of pastel will be less worked, relying more on light simple strokes.

I have seen several eighteenth-century pastel paintings, in which a small proportion of the detail was put in in gouache, which does blend well with the pastel surface, but this was clearly done for speed rather than for lack of technical effect in pastel alone.

The use of watercolour or acrylic as a base produces effects that can as well be achieved by laying and rubbing in an underpainting in pastel and setting it with fixative and, when dry, continuing with light-pressure granular strokes that leave a lattice-work of the underpainting showing through. However, the watercolour underpainting may be marginally quicker to do.

Do not attempt to use oil paint in conjunction with pastel because the canvas or board used for oils will not adequately hold the particles of pastel; and pastel papers are far too absorbent for oil paint. However, oil pastel or wax crayon can make granular marks on canvas or board and will work harmoniously with oil paint in certain circumstances.

Some very interesting effects can be made by working pastel on wet paper, although the sticks of pastel soak up a lot of the surface water. When dry the painting can be built up further, with an interesting interaction between the two applications. The dangers are that the pastel sticks can fall apart when wet and the paper may also break up.

Non-figurative composition: demonstration

I see very little essential difference between a figurative and a non-figurative painting, although in the latter case there is a purer enjoyment of shape, colour and texture for their own sakes, without the distraction of recognising objects and having to think of their association.

Whether or not you wish to work in abstract shape it is important that you employ a wide variety of textures and character of edge. In the composition on page 21 I used a piece of Bockingford NOT surface watercolour paper. I primed it with a mixture of ultramarine, burnt sienna and raw sienna acrylic paint, which I applied to the sloping piece of paper in the manner of a watercolour wash. The mixture produced a speckled pattern of deposit which settled in the indentations of the slightly rough paper, and was allowed to dry.

Detail 1 (page 20)

In this central portion I have completely obliterated the tint of the primer coat. The light blue area is rubbed in fully with the fingers and then, with a clean finger lightly travelling over the surface, the deposit of colour is partially wiped off the raised pattern of the paper, while the indentations remain filled. The dark cool grey has just the fully rubbed-in coat, but by pressing hard on the pastel stick a sharp edge is made. This area is varied by smudging or by the addition of the dividing line. The top left area is covered with a rubbed-in warm grey and the edge left flaky. I set it with fixative and then with a light pressure application of pale warm grey I bring back the pattern of the paper.

Detail 2

Apart from the filled black and yellow areas, the primer coat is visible through most of this top right portion of the painting, but it is covered with light-pressure strokes in varying colours, sometimes with the flat of the pastel and sometimes with the end. Again the character of edge is varied.

Detail 3

In this detail from the left of the painting you can see a portion of the primer coat – the mauvish speckled portion at the top left. The granulations below are light grey on a rubbed-in dark grey underlay, and a very deep green from the primer coat. Again, I smoothed some areas to give contrast.

Detail 4

The lower left detail shows variety of texture: smooth light-pressure strokes over a smoothed ground, and pointillist – that is dabbing the stick end onto the surface to achieve an irregular dot – also on a smoothed ground. I also used a variety of edge marks.

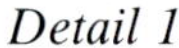

Detail 1

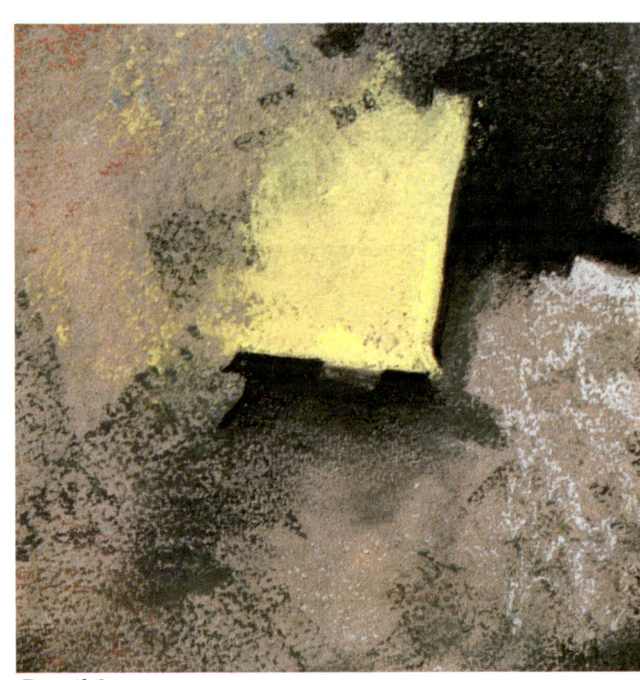

Detail 2

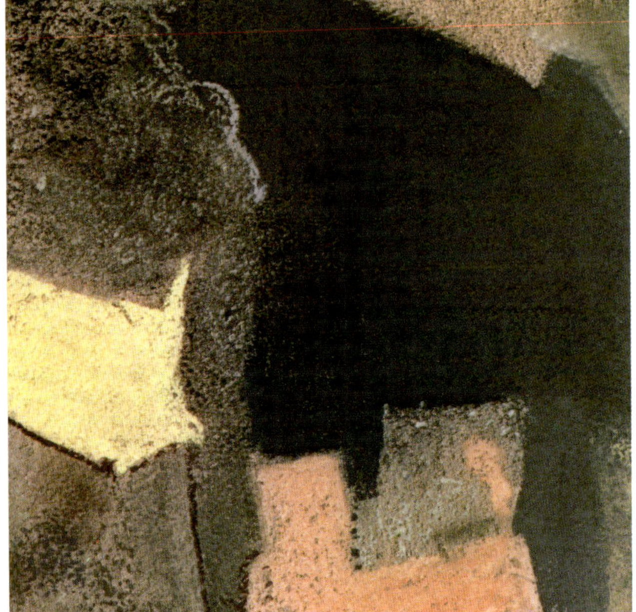

Detail 3

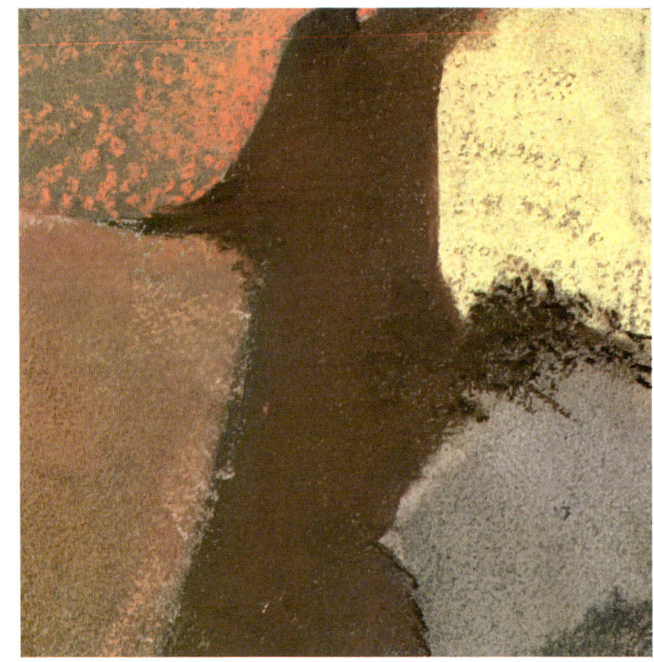

Detail 4

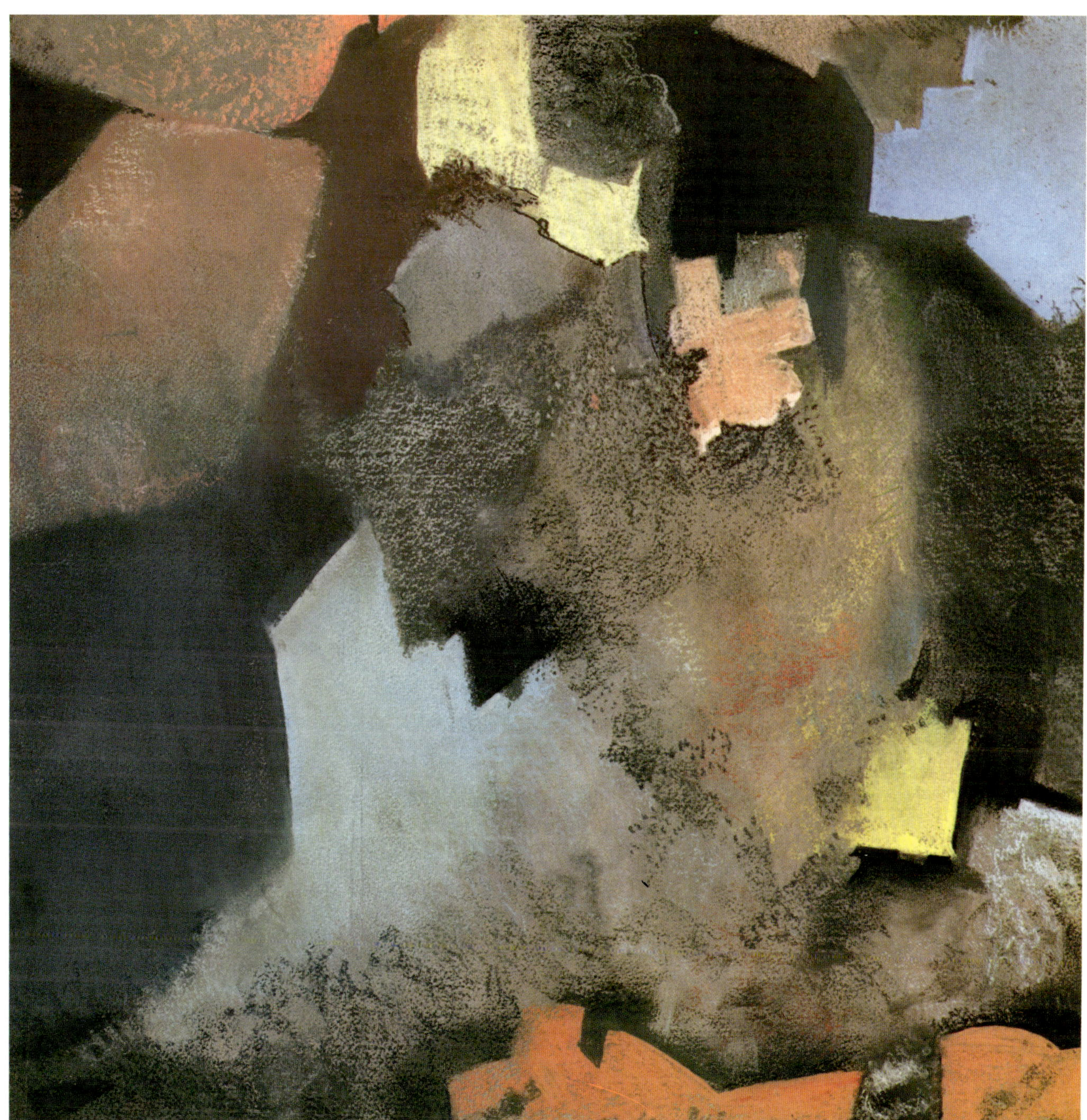

The complete painting

Church porch: demonstration of techniques

The effect of light on old stonework in the porch of a country church asks for an especially subtle range of texture, and it is a subject in which the full use of pastel really comes into its own. I used sand-grained paper as this allows me to investigate fully the worn stonework and the bands of light coming in through the open-barred door without the paper becoming overloaded and unreceptive. In the initial stages the painting was made to emerge mistily by using the same basic method as the estuary scene on pages 15–17, but it required much more textural variety and edge variation between areas of colour. I had to pay special attention to the brilliant sunlight and to surround it with sufficient shadow-depth for it to have immediate impact. Tone control was essential to the painting. Compare the monochrome photograph of the painting opposite with the same painting illustrated in colour on page 25. As you paint, concentrate on judging the interaction of tones accurately, for they are as important as the colour relationships.

Detail 1 (page 24)

The bars of light falling on the stonework were brilliantly lit and no other light in the painting was allowed to be as bright. I wanted a very sharp overall image, distorting the straightness of the bands of sunlight as they followed the shapes of stone and onto the seat area. The unlit areas had to be dark enough to emphasise the enclosed sunlight but light enough to be able to record details of surface texture. I added this textural detail after the light and dark layout had been smoothed in with my fingers.

Detail 2

I wished to portray a clearly-defined description of the door with enough irregularity to show its age. Had I wanted an absolutely perfect straight edge I would have used a template or a plastic ruler (see page 16), but instead I pressed my colours in very hard, filling the pores of the paper, and worked it in with my fingers along the grain of the woodwork I was painting. I then cut back the edge cleanly with the adjacent colour. The metal bars had been rusty at one time, and although painted now were still a little irregular, so I followed the same painting procedure as with the woodwork.

Detail 3

The side window with leaded glass was problematical, because it could demand too much attention if I made it too light. The old glass had a greenish tinge and this I made use of in playing the light down. I also darkened the recess and textured it with light strokes, leaving a granular surface.

Detail 4

Details like the brass plaque on the wall interested me, but I had to ensure again that it was treated simply enough not to detract from the centre of interest. Most of it was blocked in and smoothed before the edges and suggested inscriptions were depicted.

Opposite: the church porch painting photographed in monochrome. Compare it with the full colour version on page 25. Test whether a painting is tonally correct by photographing it in black and white. If the tones are correct in your painting, they will have the same emphasis as in the photograph, and be as convincing.

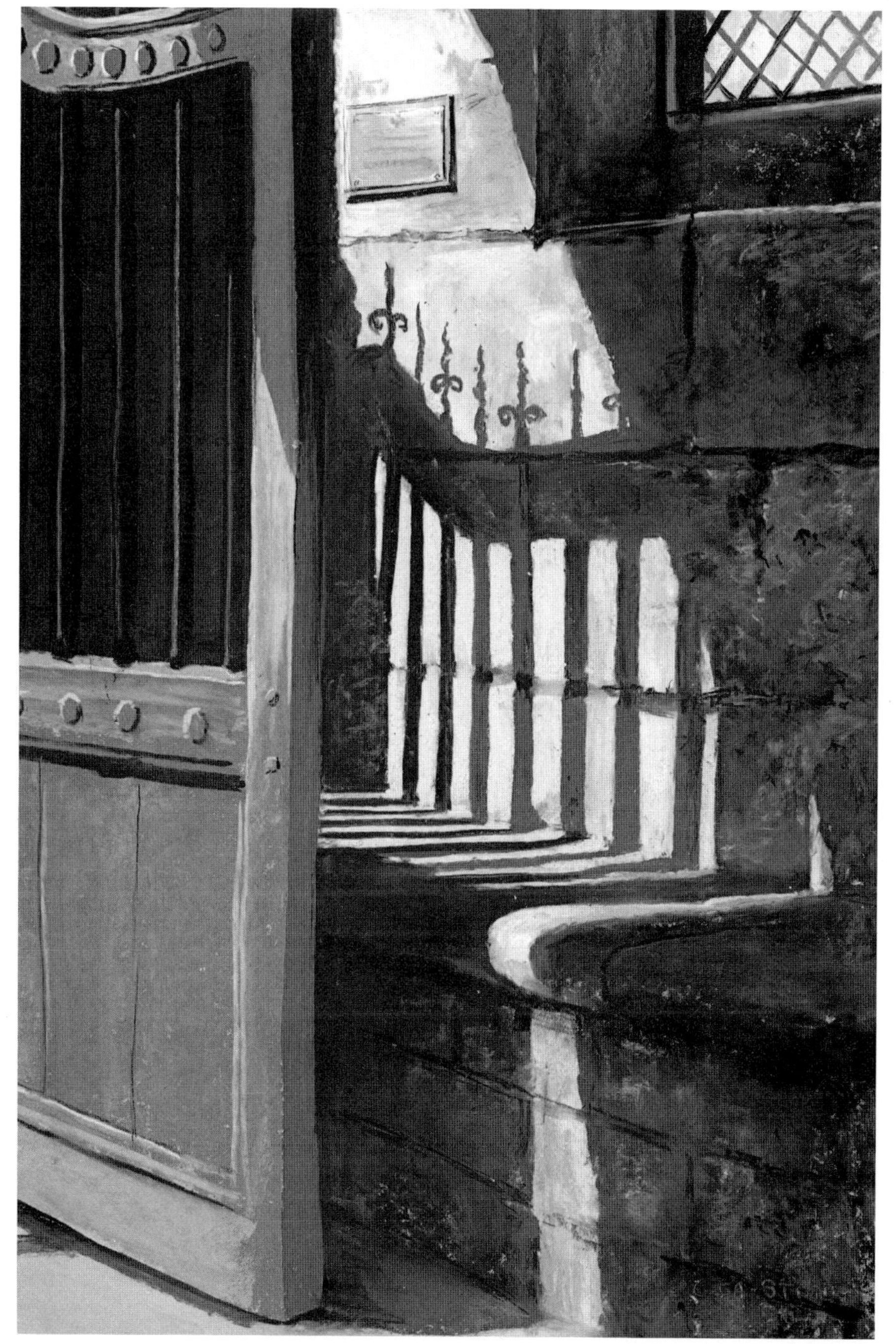

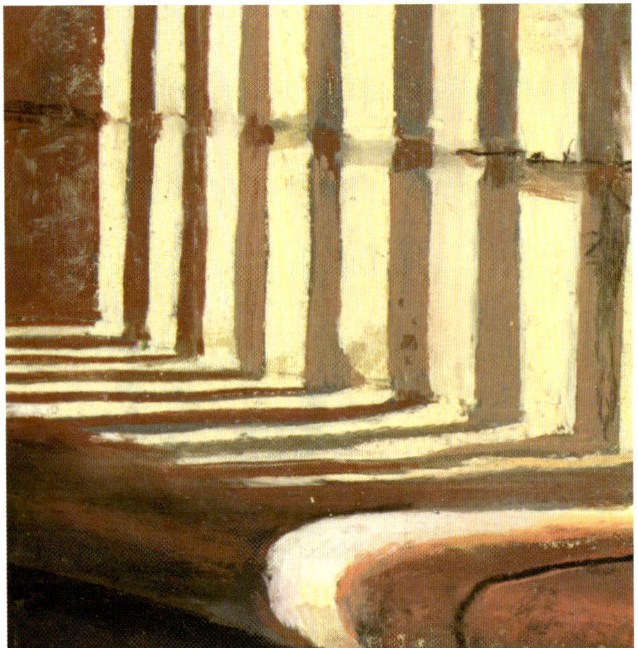

Detail 1

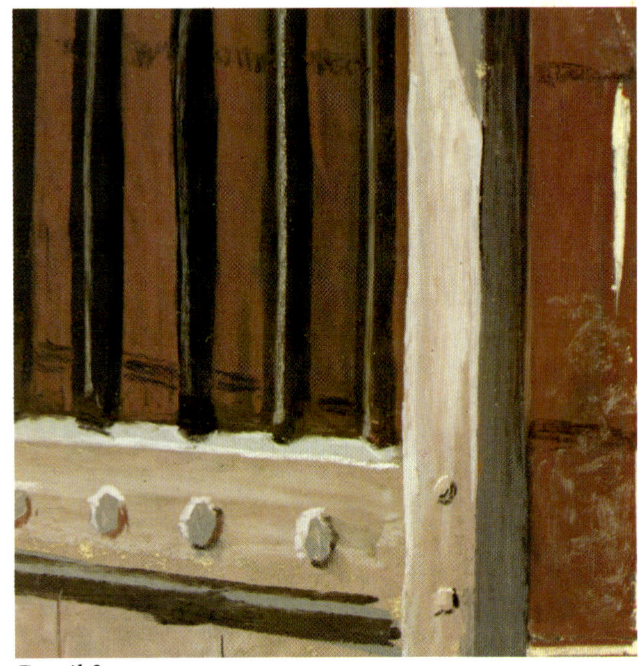

Detail 2

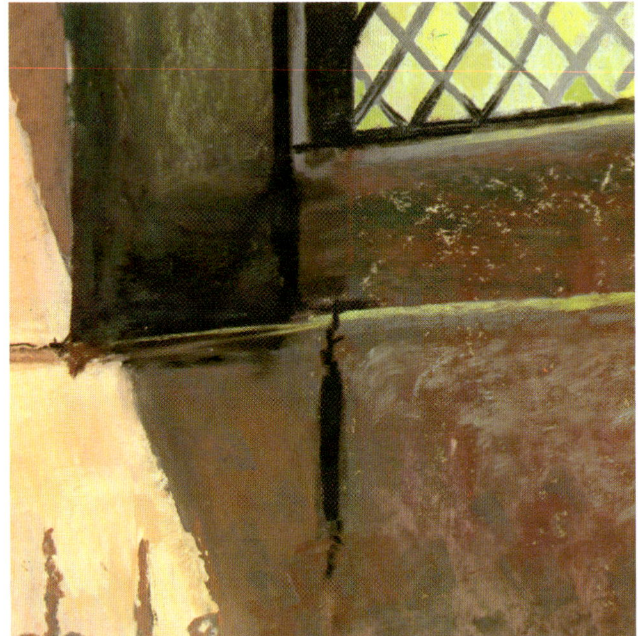

Detail 3

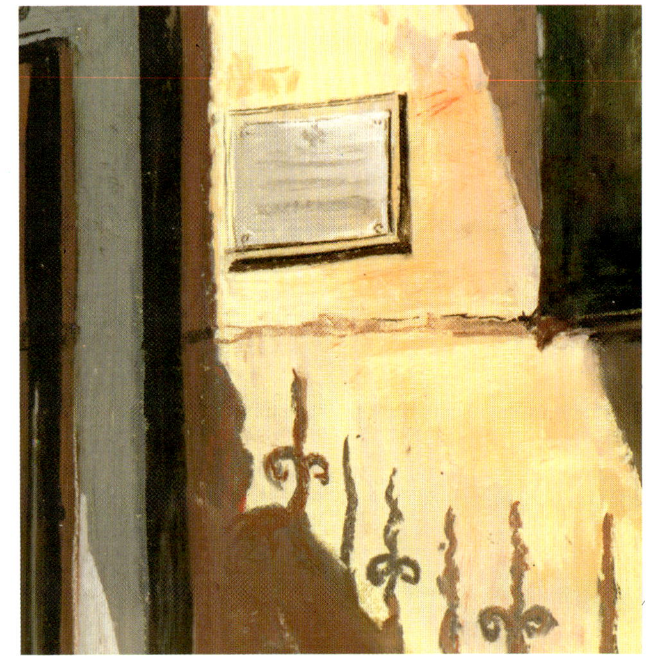

Detail 4

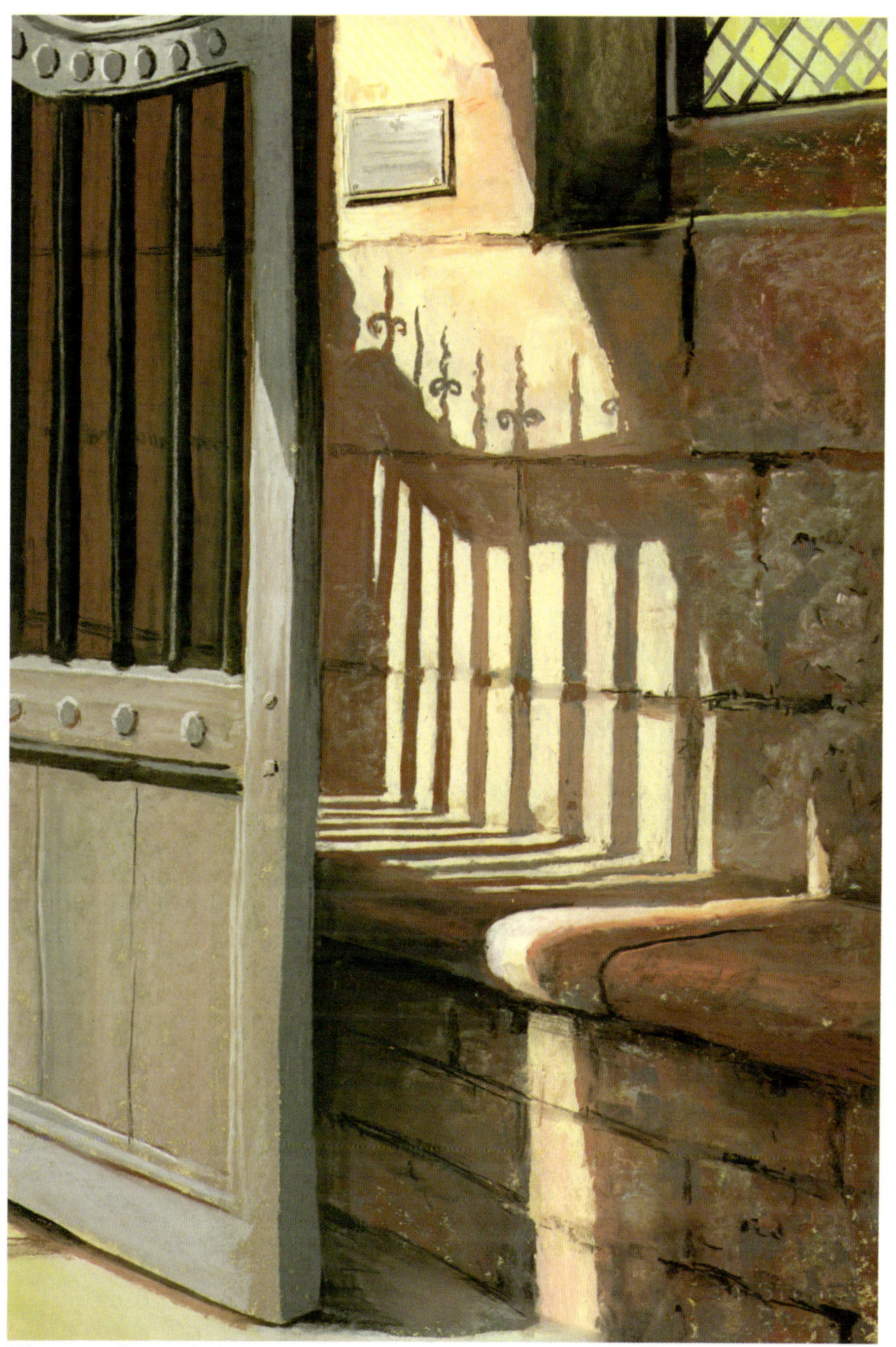

The complete painting

The sharper images in pastel

In some artistic circles it is thought that pastel can only – even *should* only – be used for misty, elusive images with little definition. However, by using a sandpaper support it is possible to achieve the definition of a perfect cut-out edge. Many abstract or super-realist painters shy away from using pastel because of their preconceptions as to what it can do. Yet it is such a powerful, versatile medium.

When I want a perfectly clear straight edge between two colours I fill the sandpaper with the one and rub it in with my fingers, so that it just overlaps the intended border line, filling the surface of the sandpaper completely. Then I lay a see-through plastic ruler or straight edge along the division I want to make. Pressing down hard on it, so that it does not move, I scrub in the second colour up to the ruler, rubbing it in as I go. Then I carefully lift the ruler and have as clear an edge as I could wish. With irregular or curved edges, cut out a piece of drawing paper to the required shape, lay it in place firmly and block in strokes from the cut template onto the sandpaper. If this is smoothed in and the template carefully lifted you will have an absolutely perfect edge. As you get accustomed to this technique, practise it freehand. I make my edges with a very heavy, deliberate freehand stroke using conté or a *medium-soft* pastel, for soft pastel tends to disintegrate with the pressure needed to fill the grain.

A perfect thick line can be ruled in with a conté stick or one of the medium-soft pastels of thin square section, or with a pastel pencil whose wood covering has been cut back to expose a length of the pastel or conté core. It is better if the line is ruled on an area that has been already laid in, as the act of filling in the adjacent shapes may well spoil the clarity of the line. Some people are reticent about using a ruler, but if an edge needs to be perfect for a certain type of painting it is less effective if it is slightly distorted by trying to do it freehand.

Motor car door: New Realist demonstration

Many people use pastel to make lovely soft romantic paintings in the traditional sense; but they may not realise that, through the techniques I have previously described, there are wonderfully powerful – sometimes intensely beautiful – images constantly presented to us in the modern world which can be effectively and dramatically portrayed in pastel.

I am fascinated by the double-image effects from glass windows, and by the bright chrome and polished paintwork on motor cars. On page 29 I show a painting of a car door. My prime interest was in the curved glass which reflected a distorted image of a line of cottages and a telephone kiosk, yet also (to a less marked extent) I could see *through* it the shape of seats within and the windows the other side. With the bodywork of the car I wanted to frame the glass area into a square shape in order to make best pictorial use of the strident interactions of shapes.

I first made a simplified construction of a car from a fairly oblique angle, and then cut this down to my square format, carefully considering the shapes of bodywork enclosed in my square and the way they would frame the window. When I was satisfied with the layout I roughly blocked the design onto the paper and then worked each area up in turn. (See opposite.)

Detail 1 (page 28)

The central area of glass was blocked in simply, just depicting the reflected image of the cottages and telephone kiosk. Once this was solidly and clearly defined (and with the paper fully covered) I started to superimpose the shapes of the seats and the other internal details.

Detail 2

I decided to define the bodywork and details of chrome trim of the car with as sharp a definition as possible. For

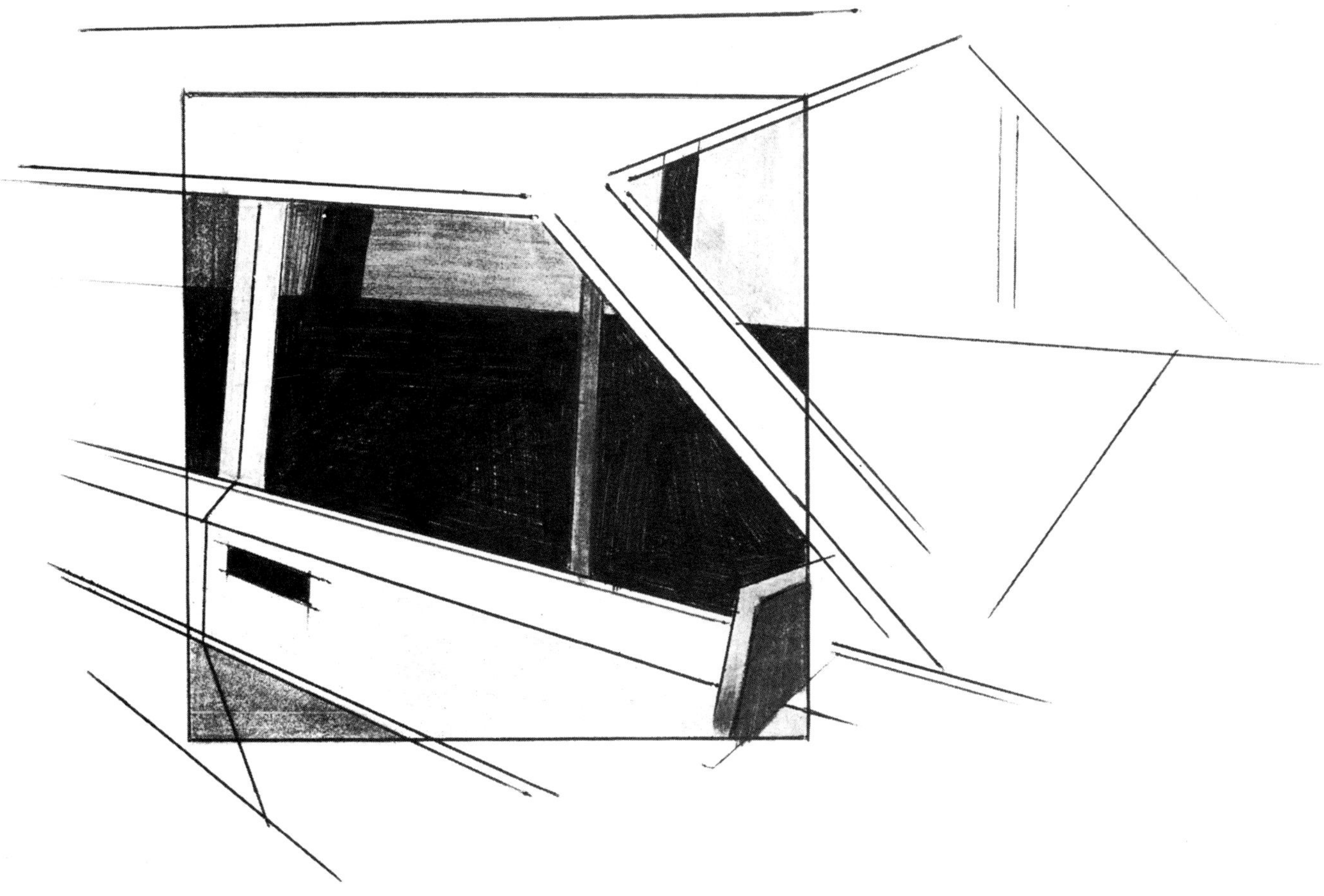

the chromework I had to put in the bands of light and dark so that some edges between them melted from one to the other defining the appropriate contours. The edges needed to be as sharp as I could make them. To obtain these I fitted the surface with pastel of the adjacent colour. Then, using a template of paper and a plastic ruler laid over in place, I cut the edge in with as heavy pressure as possible without the pastel or stick of conté breaking.

Detail 3

The metallic paint of car bodywork seems to glow rather than actually reflect, and this helped me in this composition because a complex surround would have confused the issue. The paintwork was worked in with my fingers, and then the details of door handle and chrome trim put over the top as already described.

Detail 4

Many people will leave out such details as stickers in a car window, but I find them interesting. Printed or hand-written letters or words in a painting do attract the attention forcibly however, perhaps because of our conditioning to the written word, so use them with care. Very often painters choose to use blind lettering, which gives the impression of lettering without allowing it to be legible.

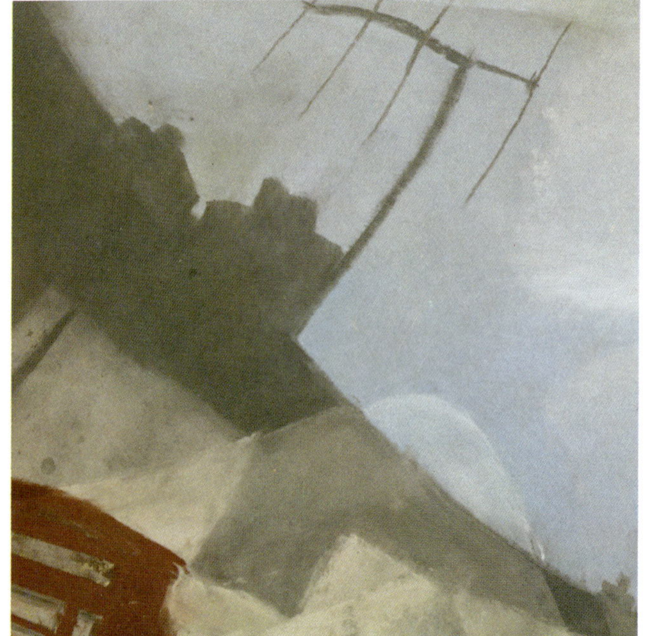
Detail 1

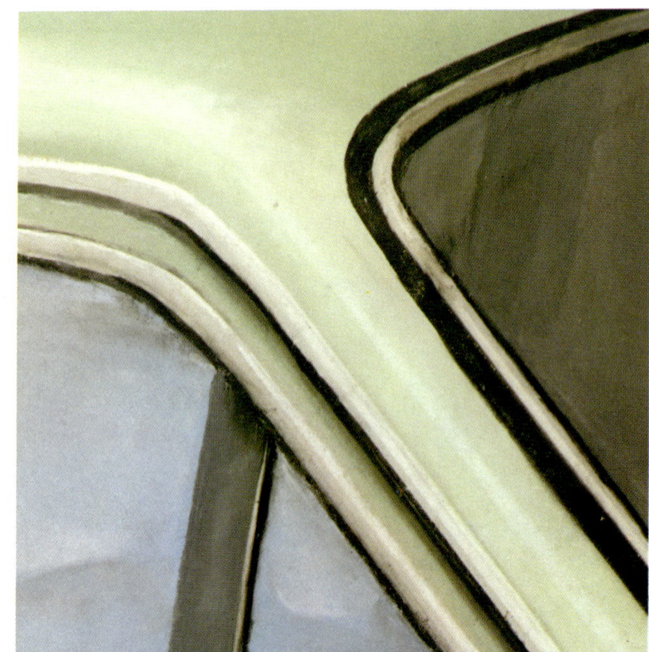
Detail 2

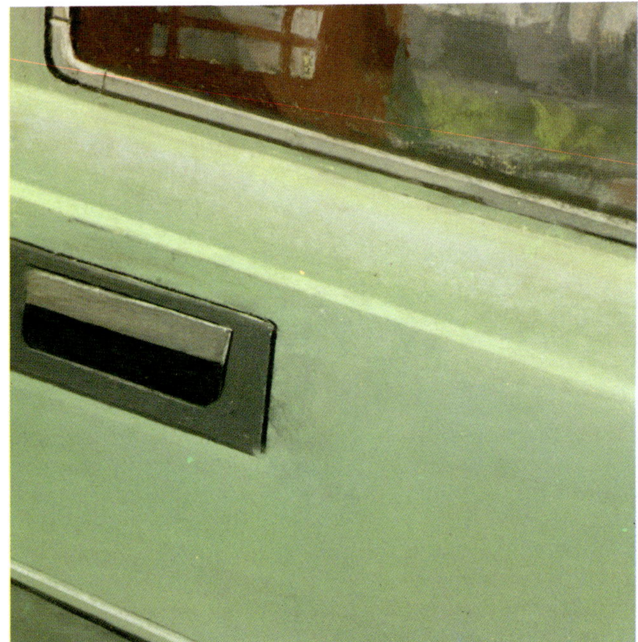
Detail 3

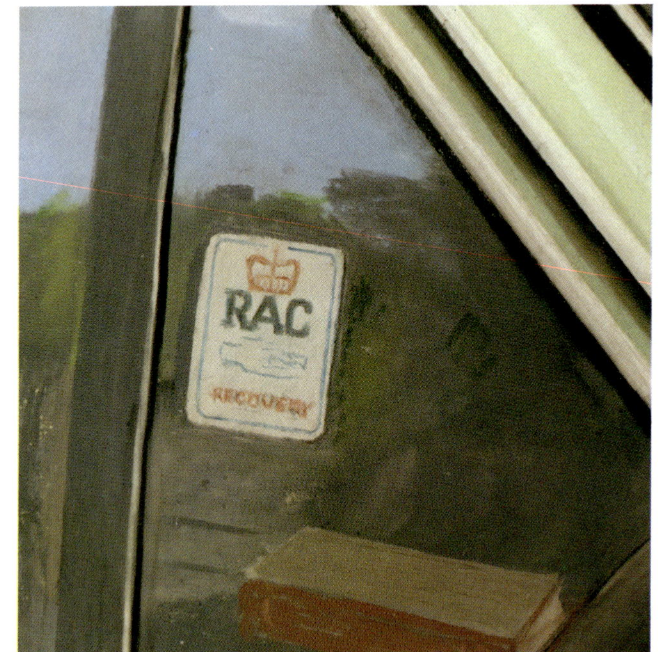

Detail 4

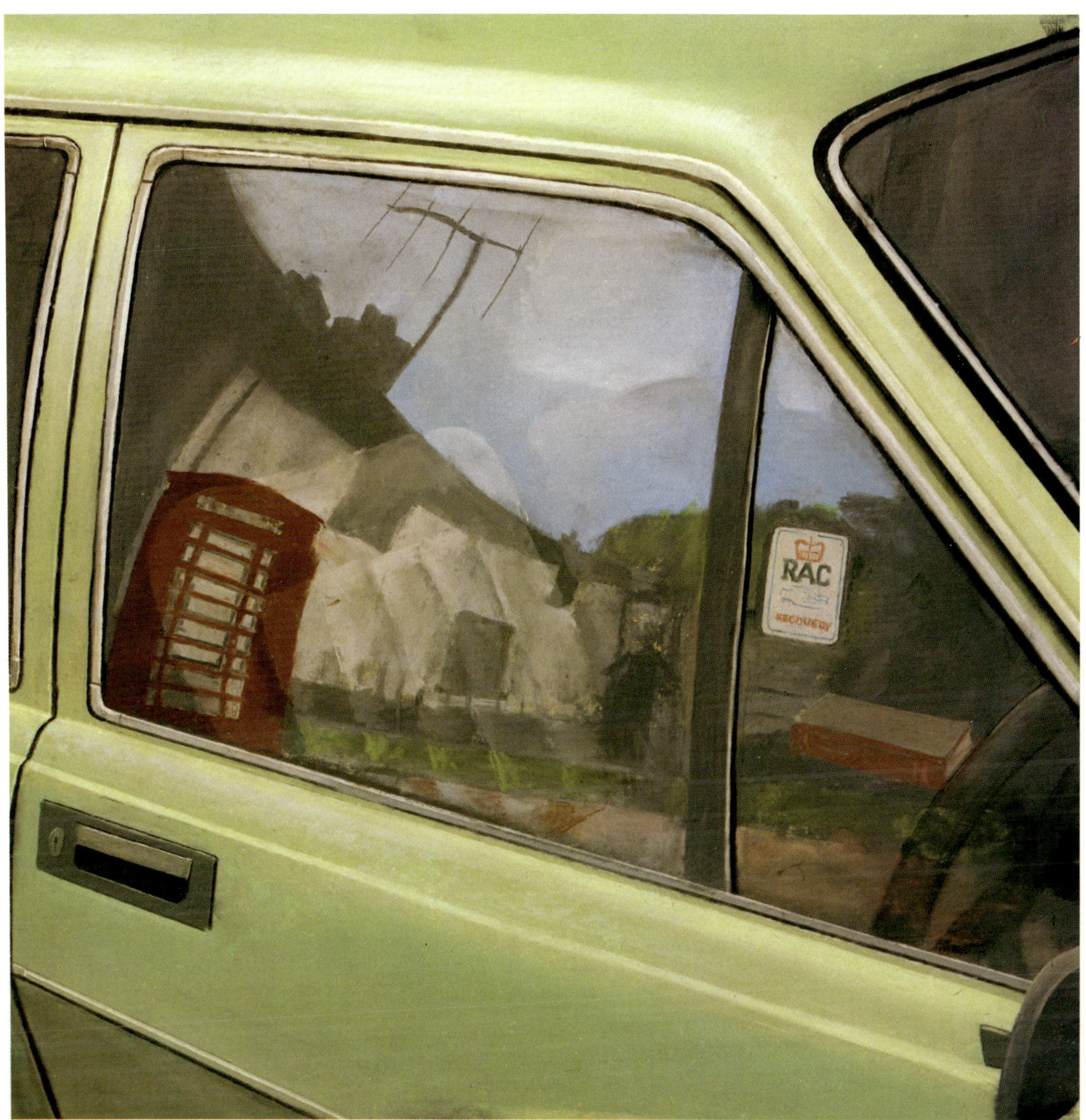

The complete painting

Storage and framing

Before they are mounted and framed pastel paintings need not cause any particular difficulty. If you are carrying a single painting still attached to your board with pins or clips, just put a covering sheet of tracing or greaseproof paper just larger than the picture over the top and secure it to the board. Polythene or cellophane sheeting is not suitable, as it lifts off some of the colour. Newspaper also takes off some of the particles of pastel, but is quite acceptable if you intend planning to do some more work on the painting later. When you are transporting several paintings these should be interleaved with tracing paper and secured in the same way, so that there can be no sideways movement. Pressure straight down onto the covered surface of a pastel painting does no harm. Sideways movement will smudge it. Longer-term storage of paintings should be treated likewise.

I am not very keen on using fixative sprayed on a finished painting, as a full spray of fixative will change the colours and tones quite noticeably, and a fine or cursory spray will not fully fix the pastel particles. I do use fixative on occasion in the course of painting (see page 18). Some pastellists who like to fix their work hang the painting with clips on a string, like washing on a clothes line, and spray the *back* of the paper, thus holding the particles of pastel down from behind. For a general note on fixatives, see page 3.

There are various schools of thought about framing pastels. Any thin paper will tend to expand and contract with the varying levels of humidity of the atmosphere, and if constricted in mount or frame will cockle with any hint of damp. Either fix the paper to the top edge of the mount only, and let it hang like a curtain, or try to keep all damp out by taping the glass to the frame and the backing board to the frame also, thus excluding all passage of air. A small painting could be actually sandwiched with no air space between two pieces of glass which are taped together at the edges, thus making an excellent seal but the extra weight of glass might be too heavy for larger paintings.

Try to frame a painting in sympathy with its general character or genre. If it is a traditional type of subject, for which you feel a mount would be suitable, I suggest

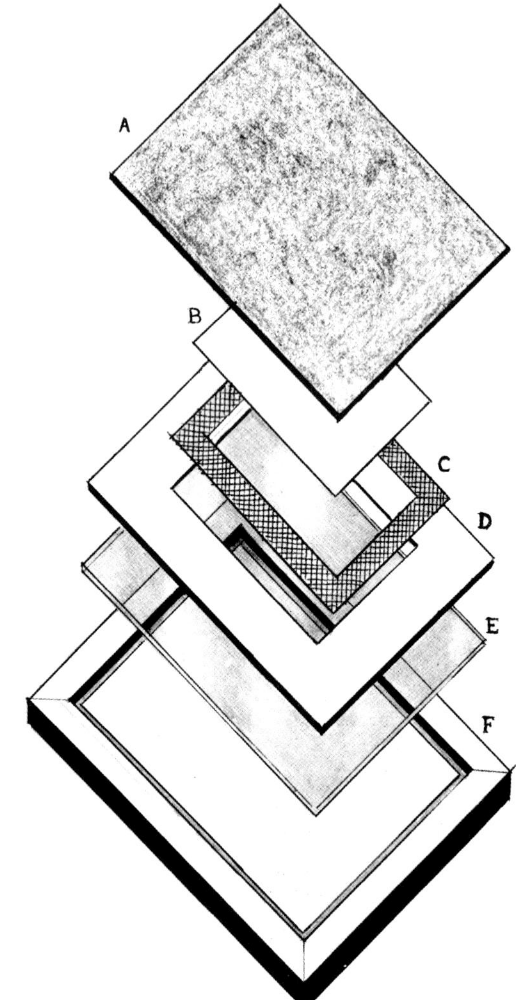

Framing

A Stiff backing board
B The painting
C Small window mount
D Larger window mount
E Glass
F Frame

If no mount or border is required and the painting is to be close-framed omit C and D, but insert a thin strip of card or wood in the frame rebate between glass and painting to separate them.

using two thicknesses of mount card in order to raise the glass well away from the picture, the inner mount having its 'window' cut slightly smaller, so that it is just visible inside the main mount. The colours of mount-card used and the width inside the frame are dictated to some extent by fashion, but it is useful if the colours echo the colours in the painting. It is better not to choose a frame or mount which is lighter than the lightest light in the picture or darker than the darkest dark; if you do you will tend to see the frame first.

Many pastel paintings of a contemporary approach can well do with an oil-painting frame. Obviously, it must have a glass; and the painting should be separated from the glass with a card or wood slip, which need not be visible inside the frame. Some paintings need only a narrow metal frame, but these too should allow an air space between the glass and the picture. This air space stops the unfixed painting touching the inside of the glass and leaving traces of the image on it. If this does happen just take the painting out, clean the glass, and reassemble.

In conclusion

I have attempted to show in this book some of the basic techniques most commonly used by pastellists, and have described the advantages and limitations of the general types of paper available. My personal aim in writing the book is to try to dispel the idea that there is any 'right' way of working in pastel. A pastel painting should not have any standardised appearance because it is pastel, nor is there any particular subject-matter that suits the medium over and above another. I contend that there is almost no type of image or effect that cannot be achieved in pastel.

I hope that you find this book useful for grasping the basic groundwork, and as a jumping-off point for further experiment. It is like learning a language: you can start with useful phrases, then string sentences together; but to become proficient in it you must actually start thinking in the language. Do use this book as a pastel phrase book and employ technique as a link between what is happening in your head and what you want to appear on your paper, not as an end in itself. Painting is about 'the seeing eye', noticing the interaction of colours and shapes all around you – often in unexpected places. The pastel medium helped me in making me really look – I am sure it could do the same, and more, for you.

ACKNOWLEDGEMENTS

Text, drawings and paintings by Christopher Stones

First published in Great Britain in 1983 by
Search Press Limited, Wellwood, North Farm Road,
Tunbridge Wells, Kent TN2 3DR

Reprinted 1986, 1989, 1991

U.S. Artists Materials Trade Distributor:
Winsor & Newton, Inc.
11, Constitution Avenue, P. O. Box 1396, Piscataway, NJ 08855-1396

Canadian Distributors:
Anthes Universal Limited
341 Heart Lake Road South, Brampton, Ontario L6W 3K8

Australian Distributors:
Jasco Pty. Limited
937-941 Victoria Road, West Ryde, N.S.W. 2114

New Zealand Distributors:
Caldwell Wholesale Ltd
Wellington and Auckland

ISBN 0 85532 524 0

Made and printed in Spain by A. G. Elkar, S. Coop. Bilbao—12

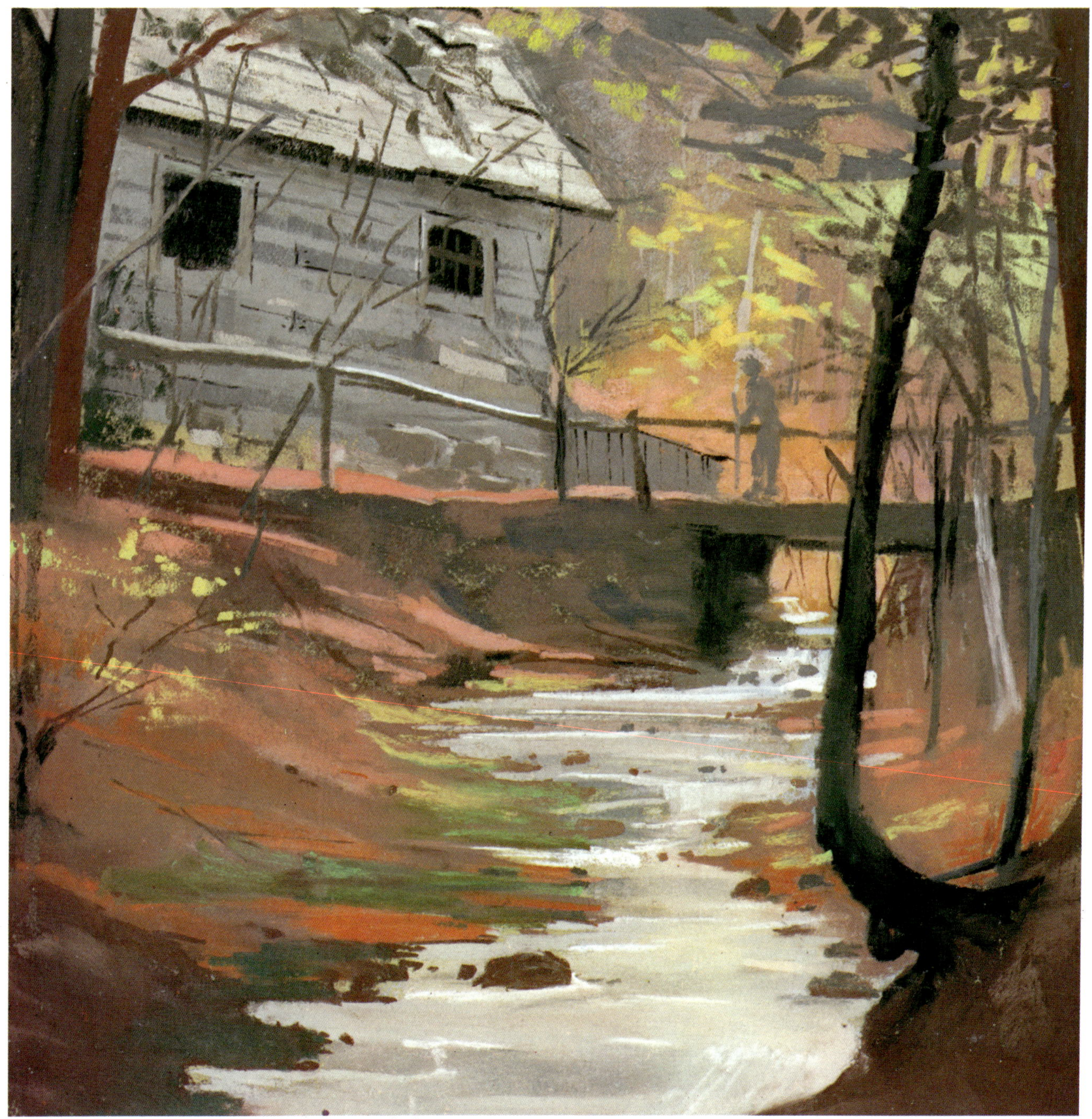

Eulenheim – Austrian woodland. See inside front cover.